Yankee Doodle Birthday
CELEBRATIONS

By Elizabeth McKinnon

Illustrated by Marion Hopping Ekberg

Warren Publishing House, Inc.
Everett, Washington

Special thanks to *Sugar Sign Press* which provided the directions for signing the words to "Happy Birthday" on p. 97. For more information about teaching sign language to young children, write: Sugar Sign Press, 1407 Fairmont St., Greensboro, NC 27403.

Some of the activity ideas in this book were originally submitted to the *Totline Newsletter* by other teachers. We wish to acknowledge the following contributors: Vicki Claybrook, Kennewick, WA; Sara Cooper, Arlington, TX; Suzanne L. Friedrich, Pittsburgh, PA; Kathie Gonion, Elk Grove Village, IL; Mildred Hoffman, Tacoma, WA; Barbara Jackson, Denton, TX; Ellen Javernick, Loveland, CO; JoAnn C. Leist, Smithfield, NC; Debra Lindahl, Libertyville, IL; Charli McClaren, Largo, FL; Joleen Meier, Marietta, GA; Susan A. Miller, Kutztown, PA; Donna Mullenix, Thousand Oaks, CA; Paula Omlin, Maple Valley, WA; Susan M. Paprocki, Northbrook, IL; Barbara Paxson, Warren, OH; Susan Peters, Upland, CA; Judi Repko, Topton, PA; Barbara Robinson, Glendale, AZ; Deborah A. Roessel, Flemington, NJ; Debbie Scofield, Niceville, FL; Betty Silkunas, Lansdale, PA; Kathy Sizer, Tustin, CA; Rosemary Spatafora, Pleasant Ridge, MI; Inez M. Stewart, West Baraboo, WI; Elizabeth Vollrath, Stevens Pt., WI; Kristine Wagoner, Puyallup, WA; Betty Loew White, Amarillo, TX; Nancy C. Windes, Denver, CO; Saundra Winnett, Lewisville, TX.

Editorial Staff: Gayle Bittinger, Susan M. Sexton, Jean Warren
Production Director: Eileen Carbary
Design: Kathy Jones
Computer Graphics: Kathy Jones, Eric Stovall

ISBN 0-911019-32-4

Library of Congress Catalog Number 90-070414
Printed in the United States of America
Published by: Warren Publishing House, Inc.
            PO Box 2250
            Everett, WA 98203

20 19 18 17 16 15 14 13 12 11 10 9 8 7 6 5 4 3 2 1

Introduction

Celebrating birthdays is a perfect way to introduce young children to famous Americans of the past whose dreams, ingenuity and hard work helped make our country great. Honoring people on their birthdays is a concept that young children understand. And when they celebrate by doing activities that relate ideas and concepts to famous people's lives, learning becomes meaningful and fun.

In this book you will find ideas for celebrating thirty all-American birthdays. Included are celebrations for twenty-seven famous people, from Presidents and folk heroes to inventors and sports figures, who lived in the past and who made unique contributions to our county's growth and character. Also included are birthday celebrations for two well known symbols — the Statue of Liberty and Smokey Bear — and for America itself. Each chapter opens with a short introduction and contains suggestions for art, music, snacks, learning games and other related activities. All of the activities are appropriate for young children and call for materials that are readily available.

Our main criterion for choosing the people to include in this book was that their lives or contributions be meaningful in some way to young children. If you work with older children, you can use the celebrations as part of larger social studies units. Or you might wish to adapt some of the activity ideas to create birthday celebrations for other famous Americans whose accomplishments would have meaning for your group.

Following are some additional suggestions to use when celebrating any of the birthdays:

- Check your local library for appropriate books about the birthday person. Set out the books and let the children enjoy looking at the pictures.
- Have the children make birthday cards for the birthday person. Arrange the cards on a table or use them to make a bulletin board display.
- Decorate a whipped topping tub or a sturdy cardboard box to resemble a birthday cake. Poke holes in the top to hold birthday candles. Each time you celebrate a birthday, bring out the cake and let the children insert the candles. Then sing "Happy Birthday" to the birthday person.
- Let each child name a special gift that he or she would like to give to the birthday person.
- Play Simon Says, substituting the name of the birthday person for "Simon."
- Supplement the ideas for the birthday celebration with activities of your own. Or let the children help decide on additional activities they would like to do.

Note: Some of the people included in this book have birthdays on holidays or have no known birthdates. You can hold their celebrations — or any of the other birthday celebrations — whenever you feel it would be appropriate.

Contents

Birthday: September 26, 1774

Johnny Appleseed

Johnny Appleseed was an American folk hero of frontier times. Born John Chapman, he spent most of his life walking barefoot throughout the Midwest, wearing a cooking pot on his head and carrying a bag of apple seeds on his back. Everywhere he went, he planted the seeds so that the settlers who came after him would have apple orchards.

Apple Printing

Cut several apples in half, some vertically and others horizontally. Remove and save the seeds to use for other activities in this unit. Pat the cut surfaces of the apples with a paper towel and allow them to dry for about an hour. Set out sheets of construction paper and pour small amounts of red tempera paint over sponges placed in shallow containers. Then let the children dip the apple halves into the paint and press them on their papers to make prints.

Paper Plate Apples

Let the children paint the back sides of paper plates red to make "apple halves." When the paint has dried, attach precut construction paper leaves and stems. Then let the children each glue a few apple seeds in the centers of the white sides of their plates.

Apple Seed Number Game

Use a red felt-tip marker to draw outlines of six apple shapes on the inside of a file folder. Number the shapes from 1 to 6 by drawing on corresponding numbers of brown seeds. Cut six matching apple shapes out of red construction paper and write the numerals 1 to 6 on them. Cover the shapes with clear self-stick paper, if desired. Then let the children take turns placing the apple cutouts on top of the matching numbered apples on the file folder.

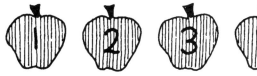

Apple Color Game

Set out different sizes of red, yellow and green apples (or use apple shapes cut from construction paper). Let the children sort the apples into three baskets according to color. Have them count how many apples there are in each basket. Then ask them to line up the apples in each group from smallest to largest.

What's Inside?

Hold up an apple and ask the children to predict how many seeds there will be inside. Cut the apple in half horizontally and let the children observe the "star" that holds the seeds. Count the seeds with the children and have them compare the number with their predictions. Try the experiment with another apple. Does it have the same number of seeds as the first one? Try the same experiment using a different colored apple.

Extension: Set out apple seeds (with several of them cut in half) and let the children examine them with a magnifying glass. If desired, provide other kinds of fruit seeds for comparing.

Five Little Apple Seeds

Place five apple seeds on the floor. Then recite the poem below with the children.

Five little apple seeds lying on the floor,
(*Child's name*) picked one up, and that left four.

Four little apple seeds, two and two, you see,
(*Child's name*) picked one up, and that left three.

Three little apple seeds, just for me and you,
(*Child's name*) picked one up, and that left two.

Two little apple seeds, oh, what fun!
(*Child's name*) picked one up, and that left one.

One little apple seed, our game is almost done,
(*Child's name*) picked it up, and that left none.

Elizabeth McKinnon

Johnny Appleseed

Johnny Appleseed Song

Sung to: "Row, Row, Row Your Boat"

Plant, plant the apple seeds,
Plant them in a row,
Just like Johnny Appleseed did,
Many years ago.

Water, water the apple seeds,
Watch them grow and grow,
Just like Johnny Appleseed did,
Many years ago.

Walk through the apple trees,
Walk through them fast and slow,
Just like Johnny Appleseed did,
Many years go.

Pick, pick the apples ripe,
Pick them high and low,
Just like Johnny Appleseed did,
Many years ago.

Elizabeth McKinnon

Applesauce

Let the children help make applesauce to enjoy at snacktime. Quarter, core and peel 3 to 4 sweet apples. Cut the quarter pieces in half and place them in a saucepan. Add $\frac{1}{2}$ cup water, sprinkle on $\frac{1}{2}$ teaspoon cinnamon and simmer, covered, until the apples are tender (about 20 minutes). Let the children mash the cooked apples with a potato masher. Then spoon the cooled applesauce into small bowls. Makes 6 servings.

Johnny Appleseed

Birthday: October 25, 1888

Admiral Byrd

Admiral Richard E. Byrd was an explorer who is remembered for the expeditions he led to the vast frozen continent of Antarctica. In 1929 he and three others made the first airplane flight over the South Pole. Later, Admiral Byrd and his party mapped new territories and made scientific studies of Antarctica's icecap and weather.

Learning About Antarctica

Show pictures of Antarctica from library books. Explain to the children that Antarctica is the coldest place in the world and that most of the continent is covered with a thick icecap. There is no life in the central part of Antarctica, but penguins and other animals live along the seacoast. Penguins are birds whose bodies are covered with black and white feathers. Instead of wings, they have flippers. They cannot fly, but they are very good swimmers.

Sparkling Icecaps

Whip Ivory Snow powder with water until the mixture is soft and fluffy. Let the children fingerpaint with the mixture on white paper plates to create "icecaps." When they have finished, let them sprinkle on small amounts of white or silver glitter. Then display the sparkling icecaps on a shelf or a table.

Penguin Puppets

Make several penguin puppets for the children to use while singing the song below. To make each puppet, cover a cardboard toilet tissue tube with black construction paper. Glue on a shape cut from plain white paper, as shown in the illustration, for the penguin's white front. Attach small white circles for eyes and glue smaller black circles in the centers. Then glue on a beak and two flipper shapes cut from black construction paper. Complete the puppet by attaching a Popsicle stick handle to the bottom of the tube.

Sung to: "I'm a Little Teapot"

I'm a little penguin, black and white,
Short and wobbly, an adorable sight.
I can't fly at all, but I love to swim,
So I'll waddle to the water and dive right in.

Charli McClaren

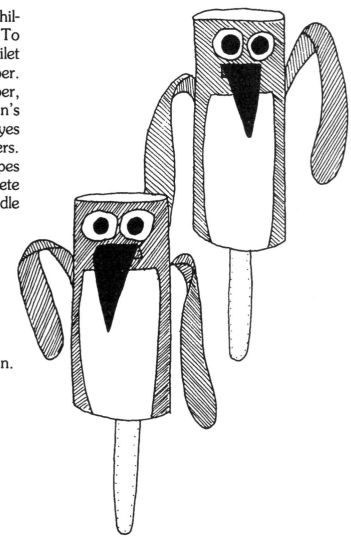

Fun With Ice

Talk with the children about how ice is the solid form of water. Then let them do the following activities:

- Put on one mitten and hold an ice cube in each hand. Which hand feels warm? Which feels cold? Why?

- Place ice cubes in paper cups. Put one cup outside (or in a refrigerator) and the others in various places around the room. Observe the ice cubes periodically. Which ones are melting the fastest? The slowest? Why?

- Sprinkle salt on ice cubes placed in small bowls and observe what happens. Then squeeze on drops of diluted food coloring (red and yellow, red and blue or blue and yellow). What happens to the colors as the ice melts?

- Float ice cubes and toy boats in a tub of cold water. Steer the boats carefully so they don't bump into the "icebergs."

A Trip to Antarctica

Collect several articles of winter clothing (a down jacket, mittens, boots, etc.) and several articles of summer clothing (a bathing suit, shorts, sandals, etc.). Have the children sit with you in a circle. As you hold up each article of clothing, have the children nod their heads and smile if it is something they would wear on a trip to Antarctica or hug themselves and shiver if it is not.

Extension: Let the children take turns choosing appropriate articles of clothing to take to Antarctica and placing them in a suitcase. As they do so, have them say, "I'm packing my bag to go to Antarctica, and in it I'm putting (a sweater/some earmuffs/etc.)."

Admiral Byrd

Freeze, Little Penguins!

Let the children pretend that they are penguins living in Antarctica. Have them line up and follow the leader as he or she waddles back and forth, slips and slides on the ice or hops into the water and swims around. After a few minutes call out "Freeze, little penguins!" and have the children try remaining in position without moving. Then choose another child to lead the line. Continue until every child has had a turn being the leader.

Admiral Byrd

Sung to: "The Mulberry Bush"

Admiral Byrd went to Antarctica,
Antarctica, Antarctica.
Admiral Byrd went to Antarctica
To see what he could see.

He saw some snow and he saw some ice,
Saw some ice, saw some ice.
He saw some snow and he saw some ice
And penguins one, two, three.

Elizabeth McKinnon

Snow Cones

At snacktime give each child a small paper cup filled with crushed ice. Slightly dilute any flavor of unsweetened frozen juice concentrate. Then pour small amounts of the juice over the ice in the children's cups to create snow cones.

Birthday: October 28, 1886

Statue of Liberty

The Statue of Liberty is a symbol of our country. For more than one hundred years she has stood on an island in New York Harbor, holding high her torch to welcome all who come to America seeking freedom. The Statue of Liberty was made in France and given to America as a gift. Her true name is "Liberty Enlightening the World."

Statue of Liberty Crowns

For each child cut a seven-pointed crown, as shown in the illustration, out of white construction paper. Use a green crayon to add windows. Let the children brush glue on their crowns. Then have them sprinkle on green glitter for a "green copper" effect. When the glue has dried, tape or staple the ends of each child's crown together.

Extension: Have the children count the number of points on their Statue of Liberty crowns. If desired, talk about how the points represent the seven seas and the seven continents of the world.

Group Statue

Set out a number of boxes ranging in size from large to small. Let the children experiment with stacking the boxes together to create a group statue. When they have finished, secure the boxes with tape. If desired, let the children paint their statue before deciding on a special place to display it in the room.

Variation: Leave the boxes unattached so that the children can use them over again to create new statues.

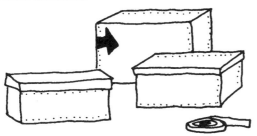

Hello, Miss Liberty

Have the children sit with you in a circle. Display a picture or a model of the Statue of Liberty. Then let each child in turn say something that he or she would like to tell the statue. Have each child begin by saying, "Hello, Miss Liberty," and be prepared to accept a wide range of topics.

Copper Cleanup

Explain to the children that the Statue of Liberty is made of copper, a metal that changes color and eventually turns green when it is exposed to air for a long time. Show them a pan with a tarnished copper bottom. Then demonstrate what happens when copper is polished by rubbing the bottom of the pan with a mixture of salt and vinegar.

Extension: Set out tarnished copper pennies and a small glass bowl containing a mixture of ½ cup vinegar and 1 teaspoon salt. Let the children drop the pennies into the bowl and observe as the tarnish disappears. Then remove the pennies and let the children polish them with small squares cut from paper towels.

How Big?

Use this activity to give the children an idea of how big the Statue of Liberty is. Let the children experiment freely with rulers, pencils and paper. Then take them outside to a large open area and mark off some of the Statue of Liberty's measurements (see below). After marking off each measurement, let the children count the steps it takes to walk that distance.

- Eye — 2 feet, 6 inches wide
- Mouth — 3 feet wide
- Index finger — 8 feet long
- Hand — 16 feet, 5 inches long
- Foot — 19 feet, 5 inches long

Extension: If desired, walk down a long sidewalk with the children, counting off 151 feet to demonstrate the height of the statue. (If you add on the height of the base and pedestal, the statue stands 305 feet tall.)

Statue of Liberty

Statue

Clear out a large space in the room and let the children play a game of Statue. Have them begin by dancing around the room in slow motion. Choose one child to be "It." When "It" tags one of the other children, have "It" freeze in place like a statue. Then let the tagged child be the new "It" and dance slowly around to find another player to tag. Continue the game until one child is left moving about. Then let that child be "It" for the next round of the game.

Lady Liberty

Sung to: "Frere Jacques"

Lady Liberty, Lady Liberty,
Standing tall, standing tall.
Holding high her torch,
Welcoming the people,
One and all, one and all.

Each time you sing the song, let a different child stand and hold high a torch made from a cardboard tube and a twist of orange crepe paper.

Elizabeth McKinnon

Torch Snacks

Purchase ice-cream cones (the kind with pointed ends). At snacktime give each child a cone to use for a "torch." Let the children fill their cones with flavored yogurt. Then let them each spoon on a swirl of whipped topping for a torch flame.

Birthday: November 6, 1854

John Philip Sousa

John Philip Sousa was America's greatest composer of marches. He was also a bandmaster who traveled for many years with his famous Sousa Band, performing concerts for people all over the world. The marches he wrote include such favorites as "The Washington Post," "El Capitan" and the rousing "Stars and Stripes Forever."

Marching Band Hats

For each child cut a 4½-inch-wide headband out of red construction paper and a 9-inch-tall plume shape out of blue construction paper. Help the children glue their plume shapes to the centers of their headbands as shown in the illustration. Have them tear blue tissue paper into small pieces and glue them all over their plume shapes to add texture. Then let them dip pieces of yellow yarn into glue and arrange them in designs on the sides of their headbands for "gold braid." When the glue has dried, staple the ends of each child's headband together.

John Philip Sousa

Marching Band Puppets

Collect cardboard French fry holders and let the children use them to make marching band puppets. Show the children how to carefully open up the holders and smooth them out flat. Let them use felt-tip markers to draw faces in the centers of the holders and to add other details as desired. Help them fold back the sides of the holders to represent shoulders. Cut two horizontal slits in the bottom part of each holder. Then weave a straw through the slits to make a handle.

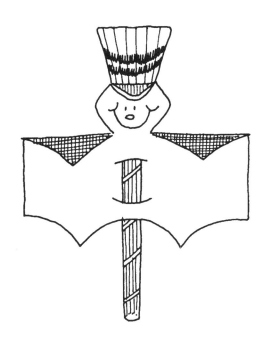

Extension: Let the children "march" the puppets while listening to recordings of John Philip Sousa's music or while singing the song on p. 21.

Learning About Band Instruments

Find pictures of band instruments in library books. Have the children sit with you in a circle. Then show them the pictures, one at a time, and let them act out how the instruments are played. Use this opportunity to teach the names of different band instruments.

Language Rhythms

Have the children sit with you in a circle. Ask each child in turn to say his or her name. Repeat the name while clapping out each syllable. Then have everyone say the name and clap out the syllables with you. Can the children identify any names that have identical rhythms?

Extension: Recite a favorite nursery rhyme while clapping out the syllables with the children.

John Philip Sousa

Rhythm Band Instruments

Let the children help make their own band instruments. Besides using the suggestions below, encourage the children to come up with their own ideas.

Drums — Use coffee cans with plastic lids placed on the ends. To make a shoulder strap for each drum, punch a hole on each side of the can at the top, poke a 36-inch piece of string in one hole and out the other and tie the ends of the string together.

Horns — Poke holes in the sides of cardboard tubes. Fasten a square of waxed paper over one end of each tube with a rubber band. To play, have the children make sounds through the open ends of the tubes while moving their fingers over the holes.

Cymbals — Use baby food jar lids for finger cymbals and pan lids for larger cymbals.

Maracas — Place rice, dried beans or pebbles in plastic eggs or bottles and seal with tape. Or tape paper cups or small cans together with popcorn kernels inside.

Wrist Bells — String jingle bells on long pipe cleaners. Then twist the pipe cleaners into bracelet shapes.

Rhythm Sticks — Use pairs of paper towel tubes, wooden spoons or short dowels. Have the children rub or tap the sticks together to make sounds.

Extension: Have the children close their eyes and listen while you play different rhythm instruments. Each time they open their eyes, have them point to the instrument you just played.

John Philip Sousa

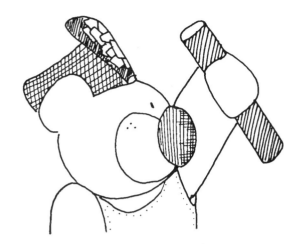

Here Comes the Band!

Have the children put on their marching band hats from the activity on p.18. Hand out rhythm instruments from the activity on p. 20. Then play recordings of John Philip Sousa's marches (or any kind of marching music) and let the children parade around the room. If desired, have the children take turns being the Bandmaster and leading the parade while moving a cardboard tube "baton" up and down in time to the music.

John Philip Sousa Song

Sung to: "When the Saints Go Marching In"

Oh, beat the drums! Oh, beat the drums!
Oh, beat them loud across the land!
Beat the drums for John Philip Sousa
And his grand old Sousa Band!

Additional verses: "Oh, toot the horns; Oh, ring the bells; Oh, clang the cymbals," etc.

Elizabeth McKinnon

Snacktime Band Concert

Let the children enjoy a pretend "band concert in the park" at snacktime. Have them pack such foods as finger sandwiches, carrot sticks and fruit slices in paper lunch bags. Then let them sit on blankets spread out on the floor and have a picnic while listening to recordings of marching band music.

John Philip Sousa

Birthday: November 25, 1835

Andrew Carnegie

Andrew Carnegie was a wealthy man who believed that everyone should have the chance to read and enjoy books. He knew that many people could not afford to buy books of their own, so he donated part of his vast fortune to help build thousands of public libraries. Today, many of the original Carnegie libraries are still in use in communities across the country and around the world.

Making Picture Books

Make a book for each child by stapling four sheets of white paper together with a colored construction paper cover. Choose a theme such as toys and write "My Toy Book" and a child's name on each book cover. Have the children look through magazines and catalogs to find pictures of toys. Then have them tear or cut out the pictures and glue them in their books. (Let younger children choose from precut pictures that have been placed in a box.) As the children "read" their books to you, write their comments on their book pages, if desired.

Variation: Let each child choose the kind of picture book he or she would like to make.

Storybook Friends

Invite each child to bring in a favorite storybook (or let the children choose books from those you have in the room). At storytime let each child hold up his or her book and tell a few sentences about it. When everyone has had a turn, sing the song below, substituting the character names from the children's books for "the Three Little Pigs."

Sung to: "The Muffin Man"

Let's sing about our storybook friends,
Our storybook friends, our storybook friends.
Let's sing about our storybook friends
Who live down Storybook Lane.

Let's sing about the Three Little Pigs,
The Three Little Pigs, the Three Little Pigs.
Let's sing about the Three Little Pigs
Who live down Storybook Lane.

Jean Warren

Mini Library

Set up a Mini Library in a corner of the room for dramatic play. Arrange books on shelves and provide a few chairs or pillows. Place a small table nearby for a library desk and let the children take turns being the librarian and standing behind it. Give each child a personalized "library card" made from posterboard. When the children find books they want to "check out," have them take the books to the librarian, show their library cards and let the librarian pretend to stamp their books (or run their cards through the computer). When they finish their reading, have the children return their books to the desk and let the librarian put them back on the shelves.

Hint: You may wish to set a limit on the number of books that can be checked out at one time.

Andrew Carnegie

Story Games

- Cut characters from a familiar story out of felt. Place the characters on a flannel-board and let the children tell the story.

- Make simple puppets to represent characters from a familiar story. Let the children use the puppets to act out the story or to make up new stories of their own.

- Make a set of story sequence cards. Let the children put the cards in order and then tell the story.

Book Shelving Game

Set out various sizes of picture books. Let the children arrange the books on a bookshelf from tallest to shortest. Then have them count the number of books on the shelf.

Variation: Attach removable circle stickers in different colors to the spines of the books (red for storybooks, blue for animal books, etc.). Then let the children arrange the books on the shelf by color.

Visiting a Library

Plan to visit a local library with the children. If possible, arrange to have a librarian talk to the children about using the library and perhaps tell them a story. Let the children spend some time browsing. Then let them help choose several books to check out and take back to the room.

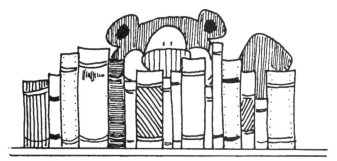

Andrew Carnegie
Sung to: "Three Blind Mice"

Andrew Carnegie, Andrew Carnegie,
Gave us free libraries.
He gave his money for you and me,
So when we go to the library,
The books we want can be read for free.
Andrew Carnegie.

Jean Warren

Story Snacks

At snacktime serve a food that relates to a favorite story. Some suggestions would be soup for "Stone Soup," gingerbread cookies for "The Gingerbread Man," oatmeal for "The Three Bears" or homemade bread for "The Little Red Hen."

Birthday: December 5, 1901

Walt Disney

From the time Walt Disney was a boy, he loved to draw. He was working as a cartoonist when he realized the potential of animation, or filmed cartoons. In the 1920s he started his Disney studio and went on to create such famous cartoon film characters as Mickey Mouse, Donald Duck, Snow White and Bambi. He also produced many popular nature and live-action movies. Perhaps Disney's greatest achievement was the creation of his spectacular amusement park, Disneyland.

Creating a Cartoon Character

Attach a piece of white paper to a clipboard and select a felt-tip marker or a crayon. Have the children sit with you in a circle. Explain to them that they will be working together to create their very own cartoon character. Start by drawing an oval or other shape in the center of the paper. Then pass the clipboard and the felt-tip marker around the circle and let each child in turn add a detail such as a head, an arm or a leg. Keep passing the clipboard around until the character is completed. Then have the children decide on a name for their cartoon character and encourage them to make up stories about its adventures.

Extension: Use the Motion Picture Notepad activity on p. 56 to help the children understand how cartoon characters appear to move when they are shown on film.

Cartoon Animal Headbands

Let each child choose a cartoon animal that he or she would like to be (a mouse, a bear, a rabbit, a pig, etc.). For each animal cut a headband and simple ear shapes from the appropriate color of construction paper. Have the children glue their ear shapes to their headbands. Allow the glue to dry. Then tape or staple the ends of each child's headband together.

Extension: Help the children put on their headbands. Then play music and let them pretend to be animated cartoon animals as they dance around the room.

Disney Sharing Table

Display Disney toys, books, records and other related items on a table. (Invite the children to bring Disney items from home to add to the display, if desired.) At circle time let each child share the item he or she brought in or choose one from the table to show and tell about. Follow up by reading one of the Disney books or playing one of the story records.

Disney Picture Games

• At a travel agency pick up identical copies of travel brochures that contain pictures of Disneyland or Disney World. Cut out pairs of matching pictures and glue them on index cards. Then mix up the cards and let the children take turns finding the matching pairs.

• Mount pictures of Disney cartoon characters on plain paper and cover them on both sides with clear self-stick paper. Trim around the edges of the pictures and cut each one into several puzzle pieces. Then set out the puzzles and let the children have fun putting them together.

Walt Disney

Building a Magical Land

Show pictures of Disneyland and talk with the children about some of the things that can be seen there. Set out materials such as blocks, small boxes, paper cups, cardboard tubes and scrap wood. Then let the children work as a group to create their own magical land by putting the materials together any way they wish.

Variation: Use disposable materials only and let the children glue them together on a piece of heavy cardboard. When the glue has dried, let the children paint their magical land as desired.

Lights! Camera! Action!

Use a shoebox and a cardboard tube to make a pretend movie camera. Cut a hole in one end of the shoebox, insert the cardboard tube and secure it with tape. Cut a small hole in the opposite end of the box. Attach the lid to the box and paint the entire camera black. Then read or tell a familiar story and let the children act out the roles of the characters. As they perform each scene, let a different child hold the movie camera and pretend to film the action.

Variation: Make a real movie by videotaping the children as they act out the story. If desired, let them paint a simple mural to use as a backdrop. Let them also choose items from a box of dress-up clothes to wear for costumes. When the taping is over, let the children sit back and enjoy watching their "movie."

Walt Disney

Walt Disney Song

Sung to: "Yankee Doodle"

Once there was a man named Walt
Whose dreams were oh, so grand.
But he worked and worked and worked,
And now there's Disneyland.
Walt Disney had a dream,
A mighty revelation,
Pictures that could move and talk —
We call it animation.

Jean Warren

Cartoon Snacks

Give each child a mound of cottage cheese on a small plate. Let the children decorate their mounds to create cartoon mice or other characters. Have them use sliced black olives for eyes, raisins for noses, carrot strips for whiskers and round crackers for ears. Let each child show his or her cartoon creation to the group before eating it.

Walt Disney

Birthday: December 8, 1765

Eli Whitney

As a boy, Eli Whitney loved learning about machines and how they worked. In the 1790s he became interested in cotton picking and processing. When he saw how long it took workers to separate the sticky seeds from the cotton fibers by hand, he invented a machine that did the job fifty times faster. He called his machine a cotton gin (a shortened name for "cotton engine"). The cotton gin helped make cotton one of our country's most important crops.

Cotton Field Mural

Place a piece of light blue butcher paper on a table. Use a brown crayon or permanent felt-tip marker to draw stems on the paper. On both sides of the stems, draw twigs with open pods growing on them. Pour glue into shallow containers and set out cotton balls. Let the children dip the cotton balls into the glue and place them all around the pods to create cotton plants. When the glue has dried, display the children's cotton field mural on a wall or a bulletin board.

Variation: Draw the stems on individual pieces of light blue construction paper and let each child make his or her own cotton plant.

Eli Whitney

Designing Cotton Fabric

For each child cut a 7- to 8-inch square out of plain white or pastel colored cotton fabric. Attach the squares to a tabletop with masking tape to prevent them from moving around. Let the children use crayons to draw designs on their fabric pieces. Then untape the squares, place them inside paper grocery bags and iron them to set the crayon. Display the decorated fabric pieces around the room. Or trim the edges of the squares with pinking shears and let the children take them home to give as gifts.

Note: Activities that involve the use of electrical appliances require adult supervision at all times.

Learning About Cotton

Show the children a picture of a cotton plant. Explain that after the plant blooms, rounded pods, or bolls, begin to form. Inside the bolls, the cotton fibers start growing out from the seeds. When the bolls are ripe, they split apart and out bursts the fluffy white cotton.

Extension: Give each of the children a fluffed out cotton ball to hold cupped in one hand. Then recite the poem below and let them act out the movements.

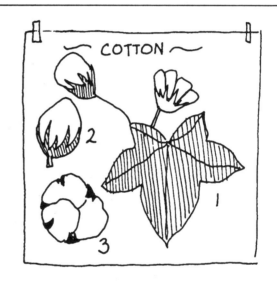

Little cotton boll
Closed up so tight.
(Close hand around cotton ball.)
Pop open now
And show your cotton white!
(Open hand to reveal cotton ball.)

Elizabeth McKinnon

Eli Whitney

Cotton Display

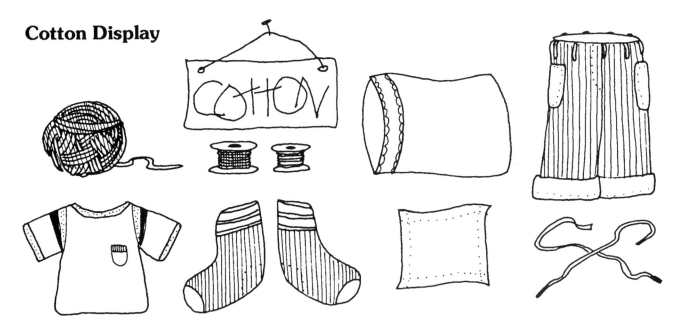

Set up a display of items made from cotton. Include cotton balls as well as such things as thread, twine, shoelaces, socks, a washcloth, a handkerchief, a diaper, a pillowcase, a pair of jeans and a shirt. You might also include a picture of a cotton plant and a real cotton boll, if one is available. Provide the children with a magnifying glass to use for examining the different cotton items.

Cotton Ball Counting Game

Place a number of cotton balls in a paper bag. Let the children each have a turn reaching into the bag and grabbing a handful. Then count together how many cotton balls each child has taken.

Variation: Let the children fill yogurt cups, plastic sandwich bags or small boxes with cotton balls. Then have them empty their containers and count the number of cotton balls that were inside.

Eli Whitney

Eli Whitney Song

Sung to: "Old MacDonald Had a Farm"

Eli Whitney made the cotton gin,
Yes, indeed, he did.
The cotton gin picked the seeds from the cotton,
Yes, indeed, it did.
It picked out the seeds, one, two, three,
It picked them out as fast as could be.
Eli Whitney made the cotton gin,
Yes, indeed, he did.

Elizabeth McKinnon

Cotton Ball Walk

Place a number of cotton balls in a small plastic wading pool. Let the children take turns walking through them in their bare feet. As they do so, ask them to describe how the cotton balls feel.

Cotton Boll Snacks

At snacktime make a "cotton boll" for each child by spooning a mound of cottage cheese into a paper baking cup. Then let the children poke raisins inside their cottage cheese "cotton" for seeds.

Birthday: December 25, 1821

Clara Barton

Clara Barton learned her nursing skills as a girl when she helped care for her brother during a long illness. After the Civil War broke out, she went to the front to nurse the soldiers, where she became known as the "Angel of the Battlefield." Later, she founded the American Red Cross, which continues today to bring aid and relief to people in need.

Red Cross Collages

For each child cut two 1- by 4-inch strips out of red construction paper. Help each child glue his or her strips to the center of a piece of white construction paper in the form of a red cross. Set out white first-aid materials such as cotton balls, cotton swabs and small pieces of gauze. Then let the children glue the materials around their red crosses to create collages. When the glue has dried, display the collages around the room.

Extension: Let the children make smaller red crosses on arm bands cut from white construction paper. Use safety pins to attach the arm bands to the children's sleeves.

Clara Barton

Good Health Charades

Have the children sit in a circle. Ask one child to stand. In the child's ear whisper the name of an activity that promotes good health, such as washing hands, brushing teeth, using facial tissue, eating nutritious foods, resting properly or getting exercise. Then have the child act out the healthy activity and let the other children try guessing what it is. Continue until every child has had a turn.

Good Health Game

Place on a tray a variety of good health items (a comb, a toothbrush, a washcloth, a bar of soap, a facial tissue, a jump rope, an apple, etc.). Have the children sit in a circle. Ask them how they feel when they are healthy and how they feel when they are not. Then let each child in turn select an item from the tray, tell how it helps him or her stay healthy and place the item in the middle of the circle. Continue until everyone has had a turn or until all the items have been chosen.

Clara Barton

Nurse's Office

Set up a Nurse's Office in a corner of your room. Provide such items as a stethoscope, a scale, cotton balls, cotton swabs, bandages and one or two white coats for the children to wear. (Make coats by trimming the sleeves and tails off old white shirts.) Let the children take turns being nurses and patients. Have them do such activities as taking pulses, giving pretend shots, listening to hearts, weighing one another and giving out healthy advice ("Get plenty of rest; Drink lots of orange juice," etc.).

Extension: For added fun, set out long gauze bandages or strips torn from a white sheet. Let the children practice bandaging the arms and legs of teddy bears or dolls.

Cotton Swab Counting Game

Number five index cards from 1 to 5. Have the children sit around a table and give them each a small paper cup containing five cotton swabs. Hold up one of the cards and have the children identify the number on it. Then have them count out that many cotton swabs from their cups and line them up on the table. Have them put their swabs back into their cups before you hold up another card. Continue the game until all the cards have been used.

Extension: Give directions such as these: "Line up three cotton swabs on the table. Place one more swab next to the first three. Count how many there are all together. Now take away two swabs. Count how many are left."

Bandage Matching Game

Collect a number of adhesive bandages in a variety of shapes and sizes. On each of five index cards attach a different set of bandages (one long and two short bandages on one card, one short and two round bandages on another card, etc.). Attach matching sets of bandages to five more index cards. Then mix up the cards and let the children take turns finding the matching sets of bandages.

Clara Barton

Sung to: "My Bonnie Lies Over the Ocean"

There once was a girl named Clara,
Who helped to make people well.
She started the Red Cross one day,
And now her story we tell.
Clara Barton, she started the Red Cross, they say.
Clara Barton, we honor her today.

Jean Warren

Red Cross Snacks

Have the children spread softened cream cheese on crackers. Then let them make red crosses on top of their crackers with small strips of red bell pepper.

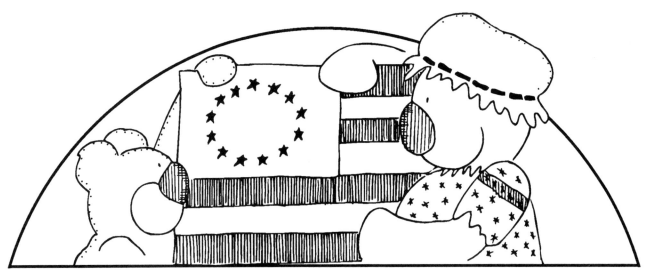

Birthday: January 1, 1752

Betsy Ross

Betsy Ross was a seamstress who lived in colonial times. It is believed that she made our country's first stars and stripes flag. The flag had thirteen white stars arranged on a blue background, and thirteen red and white stripes. The stars and stripes represented the first thirteen states to become the United States of America.

Then and Now

Show pictures of the first American stars and stripes flag and the flag we fly today. Talk with the children about how the flags are alike and how they are different. Together, count the red and white stripes on both flags. Then count the stars. Explain that the stars on the present day flag represent our country's fifty states. Follow up by asking the children to tell where they have seen the American flag displayed.

Betsy Ross

Sewing Flags

Use a hole punch to punch holes around the edges of white index cards. Give each child a card to use for a flag and a long piece of red yarn taped at one end to make a "needle." Let the children "sew" their flags by lacing their yarn pieces through the holes in their cards. When they have finished, tie and trim the ends of their yarn pieces. Then staple a plastic straw to the left side of each flag for a handle.

Extension: Let the children decorate the centers of their flags with blue crayon designs and silver star stickers.

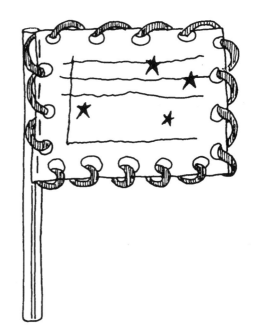

Group Flag

Select three sheets each of 9- by 12-inch red, white and blue construction paper. Cut the papers in half to make eighteen "squares." Set out a box of red, white and blue collage materials (buttons, yarn, ribbon, beads, fabric scraps, etc.). Give the children the construction paper squares and let them glue on matching colored collage items. Attach the squares in three rows to a sheet of butcher paper to create an 27- by 36-inch flag. Add a strip of dark colored construction paper for a flagpole. Then display the flag on a wall or a bulletin board.

Variation: Instead of using collage materials, let the children glue on small pieces of matching colored tissue paper.

Thirteen Stars

Betsy Ross's flag is often pictured as having the stars arranged in a circle. Use her design to teach or review the number 13. For each child draw thirteen dots in a circle on a sheet of blue construction paper. Give each of the children thirteen silver star stickers and let them attach the stars to the dots on their papers. When they have finished, have them count their stars. Then write the numeral 13 at the bottom of each paper.

Betsy Ross Song

Sung to: "Frere Jacques"

Betsy Ross, Betsy Ross,
We thank you; yes, we do.
You made our country's flag,
With its stars and stripes,
Red, white, blue; red, white, blue.

Elizabeth McKinnon

Matching Flags

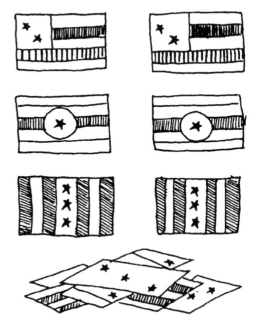

Select ten white index cards and divide them into pairs. Use red and blue felt-tip markers and star stickers to create matching flag designs on each pair. If desired, staple a plastic straw to the left side of each flag for a handle. Then mix up the flags and let the children take turns finding the matching pairs.

Variation: Purchase sets of miniature flags from different countries (available at craft and variety stores). Let the children use the flags for matching and counting games.

Flag Parade

Hand out several small American flags. Talk with the children about how we honor our flag by holding it with respect and never letting it touch the ground. Then sing the song below and let the children march around the room in a Flag Parade. Have them take turns holding the flags and leading the line.

Sung to: "Row, Row, Row Your Boat"

Wave, wave, wave the flag,
As we march around.
Hold it high to show our pride,
It must not touch the ground.

Wave, wave, wave the flag,
Dear red, white and blue.
Stars and stripes forever bright,
America — to you!

JoAnn C. Leist

Graham Cracker Flags

At snacktime mix softened cream cheese with a small amount of unsweetened frozen apple juice concentrate. Let the children make "flags" by spreading the cheese on graham crackers. Then let them decorate their flags by placing strawberry slices and blueberries on

Birthday: January 15, 1929

Martin Luther King, Jr.

Martin Luther King, Jr. was a civil rights leader who devoted his life to the nonviolent struggle for peace and freedom for all people. Dr. King had many dreams for his country. One of those dreams was that his four children would "one day live in a nation where they will not be judged by the color of their skin but by the content of their character." Another dream was that all children, no matter what their race or religion, would someday be able to join hands and become friends.

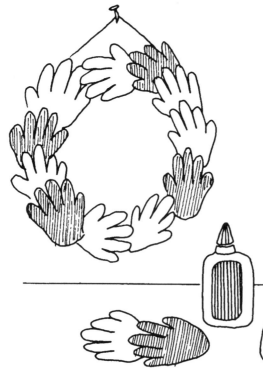

Friendship Wreath

Give each child a sheet of construction paper in the color of his or her choice. Let the children help one another trace around their right and left hands on their papers. Have them each cut out their own hand shapes (or cut them out yourself). Cut a wreath shape from posterboard and place it on a table or on the floor. Then let each child glue his or her hand shapes to a section of the wreath. When the glue has dried, display the children's "friendship wreath" on a wall or a bulletin board.

Martin Luther King, Jr.

Handprint Placemats

Let the children make handprint placemats to use for snacktime. Give each child a large sheet of construction paper. Spread thick tempera paint on a sheet of heavy plastic. Then let the children place their hands in the paint and press them all over their papers to make handprints. When the paint has dried, cover the placemats with clear self-stick paper, if desired.

I Have a Dream

Martin Luther King is remembered for his "I Have a Dream" speech in which he wished for a country where all people would live together in harmony. Talk with the children about dreams, or wishes. What things could they wish for that would make our country a better place for everyone to live? If desired, write the children's wishes on paper for them to illustrate. Then fasten the papers together with a cover to make an "I Have a Dream" book.

What If?

Talk with the children about how Martin Luther King believed that we should try to solve our problems peacefully. Then ask "What if?" questions about problems that commonly arise and help the children to come up with peaceful solutions. For example, ask: "What if you want to play on the swing but your friend won't get off? What if you're starting a game and both you and your friend want to be first? What if there's one cookie left and three of you want it?" Encourage the children to bring up other problems for the group to try solving.

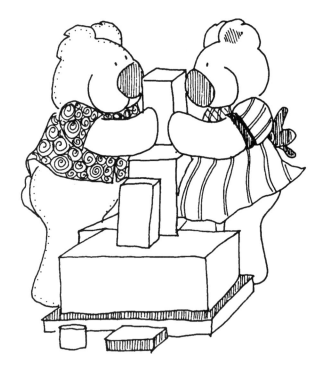

Cooperative Learning Activities

Divide the children into small groups. Then let them take turns doing the cooperative learning activities below.

*   Give each of the children a block or a box and let them work together to build a spaceship, a skyscraper or some other structure.

*   Cut a large posterboard shape into puzzle pieces. Give a piece to each of the children and let them put the puzzle together.

*   Give each child a circle, a square and a triangle cut from felt. Let the children work together to create a clown, an animal, a car or other object by placing their shapes on a flannelboard.

Peace March

Have the children find partners and hold hands. Then let them march around the room while singing the song below.

Sung to: "When Johnny Comes Marching Home"

Let's all go marching hand in hand
For peace today.
Let's all go marching hand in hand,
We'll shout "Hurray!"
For Dr. King we will march along,
And to make our country strong,
We'll go hand in hand
Together, one and all.

Jean Warren

Martin Luther King, Jr.

Brotherhood

Sung to: "Mary Had a Little Lamb"

Brotherhood for you and me,
You and me, you and me.
Brotherhood for you and me,
Taught Martin Luther King.

We should live in harmony,
Harmony, harmony.
We should live in harmony,
Taught Martin Luther King.

Debra Lindahl

Friendship Soup

Invite each child to bring a vegetable from home to use for making soup. (Suggested vegetables would be carrots, potatoes, tomatoes, celery, onions and zucchini.) Help each child peel his or her vegetable and chop it into pieces. Pour water into a large pot and let the children add their vegetables. Bring the water to a boil and add instant broth or bullion. Simmer, covered, for about 45 minutes or until the vegetables are tender. Then season to taste and let the children enjoy their "friendship soup" at snacktime.

Variation: Give each child a different kind of fruit to help prepare for making a "friendship salad."

Birthday: January 17, 1706

Benjamin Franklin

Benjamin Franklin was a man of many talents. Besides being a diplomat, he was a printer, an author, an inventor and a scientist. He wrote and printed his own newspaper as well as an almanac that contained wise sayings we still use today. His inventions included bifocal eyeglasses and the Franklin stove. Perhaps he is best remembered for flying a kite in a thunderstorm to prove that lightning is a form of electricity. This experiment led him to invent the lightning rod.

Decorated Kite Pictures

Give each child a kite shape (about 7 inches long) cut from white construction paper and folded in half lengthwise. Have the children open their shapes and use eyedroppers to squeeze drops of tempera paint on one of the sides. Have them refold their kites, rub over them gently with their hands and then open them to see the designs they created. When the paint has dried, let the children glue their kites, along with pieces of yarn for kite strings, on sheets of dark blue construction paper.

Extension: If desired, talk with the children about the key that Benjamin Franklin tied to the string of his kite when he made his famous experiment. Then give them key shapes cut from gold wrapping paper to add to their kite pictures.

Printing Newspapers

Let the children have fun printing their own "newspapers." Collect a number of rubber stamps that contain words (address stamps, old or outdated office stamps, etc.). Set out the stamps, along with several black ink pads. Give each child a folded piece of white construction paper or newsprint. Then let the children press the stamps on the ink pads and use them to print words on the pages of their newspapers.

Far and Near

Talk with the children about the bifocal eyeglasses that Benjamin Franklin invented. Explain that the lenses were special because they allowed him to see clearly both far and near. Have the children pretend to put on Benjamin Franklin glasses. Then have them sit in a group on one side of the room. Place several toys or other objects on the opposite side of the room and several close by. Start the game by saying, "I see something far from me that is red and round. What is it?" (A ball.) Keep giving clues until the children guess what the object is. Then say, "I see something near me that is brown and fuzzy and has two eyes. What is it?" (A teddy bear.) Continue the game by letting the children take turns giving clues about objects that are far and near.

Wise Sayings

Benjamin Franklin is remembered for his many wise sayings such as "A penny saved is a penny earned," and "A word to the wise is enough." Let the children have fun repeating the following rhyme:

Early to bed and early to rise,
Makes a man healthy, wealthy and wise.

Benjamin Franklin

Kite Matching Game

Use felt-tip markers to draw a kite on each of five large index cards. Add a tail to each kite. Draw one small bow on one kite tail, two small bows on another kite tail and so on. Select five more index cards and number them from 1 to 5. Mix up the cards and place them in a pile. Then let the children take turns matching the kite cards with the numbered cards by counting the bows on the kite tails.

Variation: Draw matching pairs of different colored or patterned kites on the index cards.

Franklin Stove

Use a cardboard carton to make a pretend Franklin stove. Cut all but one of the top flaps off the carton and cover a table with newspaper. Place the carton on its side with the flap opened out on top of the newspaper. Let the children paint the carton black, inside and out. When the paint has dried, place the stove on the floor between two chairs set against a wall for a "fireplace." Have the children arrange small pieces of wood and crumpled orange tissue paper in the back of the stove for a fire. Then let them enjoy sitting around their stove at storytime or snacktime.

Extension: If possible, show a picture of a Franklin stove. Talk about how the cast iron "box" helps to send heat out into the room and prevent it from escaping up the chimney.

Benjamin Franklin

Benjamin Franklin Song
Sung to: "Old MacDonald Had a Farm"

Benjamin Franklin flew a kite,
Way up in the sky.
He flew it in a thunderstorm,
Flew it, oh, so high.
His kite went up, his kite went down,
His kite went twirling all around.
Benjamin Franklin flew a kite,
Way up in the sky.

Elizabeth McKinnon

Kite Sandwiches
Cut bread and cheese slices into kite shapes.
Let the children spread mayonnaise on the
bread, if desired. Then let them put the bread
and cheese slices together to make kite sandwiches for snacktime.

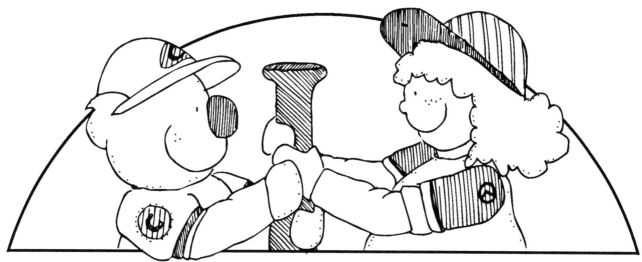

Birthday: January 31, 1919

Jackie Robinson

Jackie Robinson was one of America's greatest professional baseball players. Born Jack Roosevelt Robinson, he grew up playing many sports. In 1947 he joined the Brooklyn Dodgers and went on to help his team win six National League pennants as well as the 1955 World Series. Jackie Robinson was elected to the Baseball Hall of Fame in 1962. He is remembered for his great athletic skills, his fine character and for the pathway he paved for minorities to enter professional sports.

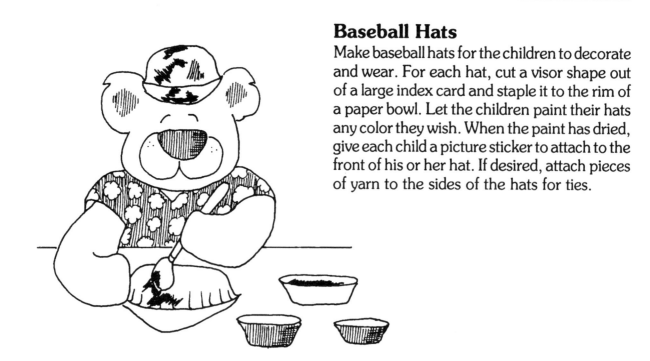

Baseball Hats

Make baseball hats for the children to decorate and wear. For each hat, cut a visor shape out of a large index card and staple it to the rim of a paper bowl. Let the children paint their hats any color they wish. When the paint has dried, give each child a picture sticker to attach to the front of his or her hat. If desired, attach pieces of yarn to the sides of the hats for ties.

Diamond Collages

Cut different sizes of diamond shapes from various colors and kinds of paper (construction paper, wrapping paper, wallpaper, etc.). Give each child a number of shapes, along with a sheet of construction paper and some glue. Then let the children glue their shapes all over their papers to create diamond collages.

Baseball Card Fun

Use a set of baseball cards to do the following activities with the children:

- Spread out the cards on a table or on the floor. Ask the children to find pictures of players at bat, players pitching balls, players wearing mitts, etc. Or hold up different cards and ask the children to tell what the players are doing.

- Point out the team logos on the cards. Are any of the players on the same teams or are they all on different teams? Ask the children to compare the uniforms of the different teams. How are they alike? How are they different?

- Give each child a different number of baseball cards. Have each child in turn count out his or her cards and place them in a central pile. Then count how many cards there are all together.

Extension: Let the children make up their own games to play with the baseball cards.

Flannelboard Baseball Game

Cut five baseball mitt shapes out of brown felt. Along the bottom edges of the shapes, glue small circles cut from black felt to number the mitts from 1 to 5. Cut five circles out of white felt for baseballs. Number the baseballs from 1 to 5 by gluing on felt numerals. Place the mitts on a flannelboard. Then let the children take turns placing the baseballs on the matching numbered mitts.

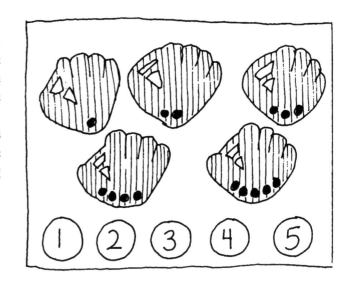

Baseball Directions Game

Divide the children into small groups and let them take turns playing this game. Tape four squares of construction paper to the floor to represent bases on a baseball diamond. Walk around the bases with the children, naming each one as you go. Then stand in the middle of the diamond and have the children line up outside it. When the first child in line walks up and stands on home base, "pitch" him or her a direction such as "Hop to first base." Continue with other directions such as "Skip to second base; Tiptoe to third base; Gallop to home base." After the child has gone around the bases, declare a "home run." Follow the same procedure until every child has had a turn.

Jackie Robinson

Batter Up!

Take the children outside and let them have fun playing baseball with a plastic ball and bat. Have them take turns batting and pitching (or pitch the ball yourself if the children in your group are very young). When a child makes a hit, let him or her run to a designated spot and back again. Continue the game as long as interest lasts.

Hint: If you have a large group, provide several plastic balls and let the children who are waiting their turns "warm up" by playing catch.

Jackie Robinson

Sung to: "Frere Jacques"

Jackie Robinson, Jackie Robinson,
Went to bat, went to bat.
   (Hold pretend bat over shoulder.)
He hit a home run,
   (Swing pretend bat.)
He hit a home run,
Just like that, just like that!

Continue singing the song, each time substituting a child's name for "Jackie Robinson."

Elizabeth McKinnon

Mini Hot Dogs

Let the children help make mini hot dogs for snacktime. Give each child a refrigerator biscuit and one-half of a hot dog. Let the children flatten their biscuits on a clean surface. Then have them wrap their biscuits around their hot dog halves and place them on a cookie sheet. Bake for 10 minutes at 400 degrees. Serve with small cups of lemonade, if desired.

Birthday: February 11, 1847

Thomas Edison

Thomas Alva Edison was a great inventor. Even as a young child, he loved to experiment and discover how things worked. He invented many of the things we use today, such as the light bulb, the phonograph, the microphone and the motion picture camera. In all, Thomas Edison patented more than one thousand inventions.

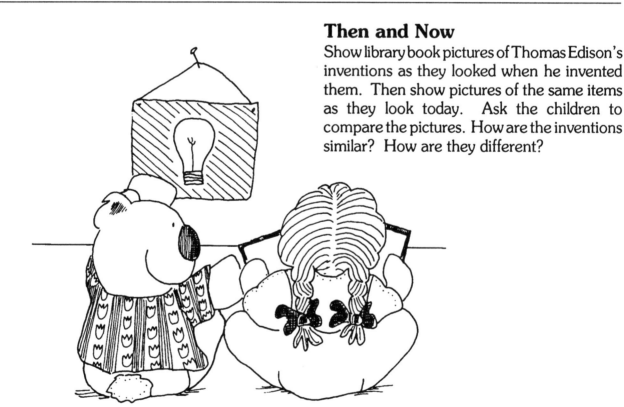

Then and Now

Show library book pictures of Thomas Edison's inventions as they looked when he invented them. Then show pictures of the same items as they look today. Ask the children to compare the pictures. How are the inventions similar? How are they different?

Phonograph Art

For this activity you will need an old record player (any kind will do as long as the turntable still spins), construction paper circles the size of long-playing records, two or three squeeze bottles filled with different colors of tempera paint and lots of newspapers. Cover a low table and the floor around it with newspapers and put the record player on the table. Help one child at a time place a construction paper circle on the turntable. Turn on the record player. Then let the child gently squeeze paint onto the spinning circle to create "phonograph art."

Variation: Instead of using paints, let the children hold felt-tip markers on the spinning circles.

Recording Voices

Thomas Edison's phonograph gave people the opportunity to record and play back voices for the first time. Use a tape recorder (preferably one with a hand-held microphone) to record the children as they tell you their names and something about themselves. If necessary, ask them questions such as "How old are you? What is your favorite game? What do you like to eat?" Then play back the tape and let the children listen to their voices.

Light Bulb Puzzles

Number the left-hand sides of five large index cards from 1 to 5. Draw corresponding numbers of light bulbs on the right-hand sides of the cards. Cut each index card into two puzzle pieces. Then place all the pieces in a pile and let the children take turns finding the match-ups.

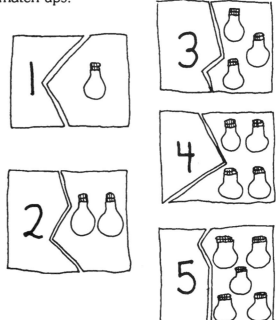

Thomas Edison

Motion Picture Notepad

To make a simulation of a motion picture, you will need a blank notepad that contains at least ten to fifteen pages. Hold the pad so that the binding is on the left. Draw a snowflake (or other simple object) at the top of the first page about 2 inches from the right-hand side. On the second page, draw an identical snowflake slightly down and to the right of where it was on the first page. Continue on each page until the snowflake is at the bottom right-hand corner. Let the children take turns making the snowflake "fall" by holding the notepad in one hand and flipping through the pages with the other.

Light the Bulb

Make one or more light bulb sets for the children to experiment with. For each set, you will need one "D" size battery, a 1- by 6-inch piece of aluminum foil, a flashlight bulb and transparent tape. Tear off a 6-inch piece of tape and place it down the middle of the dull side of the aluminum foil. (This makes the foil sturdier.) Fold the foil in thirds lengthwise. Tape one end of the foil strip to the flat end of the battery and stand the battery on a table. To light the bulb, have the children hold it upright on top of the battery and touch the loose end of the foil strip to the bulb's metal side.

Oh, Edison

Sung to: "When Johnny Comes Marching Home"

Oh, Edison made the light bulb,
Hurray, hurray!
Oh, Edison made the light bulb,
Hurray, hurray!
He liked to plan out things to do,
And then invent something new.
And we're all so glad
That Edison worked so hard!

Repeat, substituting the names of Edison's other inventions for the word "light bulb."

Jean Warren

Snacktime Experiment

Waxed paper was one of Thomas Edison's many inventions. Let the children help make peanut butter sandwiches early in the day and wrap them in waxed paper for eating later. Set out an unwrapped piece of bread at the same time. At snacktime let the children compare the bread in their sandwiches with the unwrapped piece of bread to observe how the waxed paper helped keep their sandwiches from drying out.

Note: Activities that involve the use of electrical appliances require adult supervision at all times. Although the activities in this unit are safe to do, remind the children that they should never touch light bulbs or other electrical objects without an adult's permission.

Thomas Edison

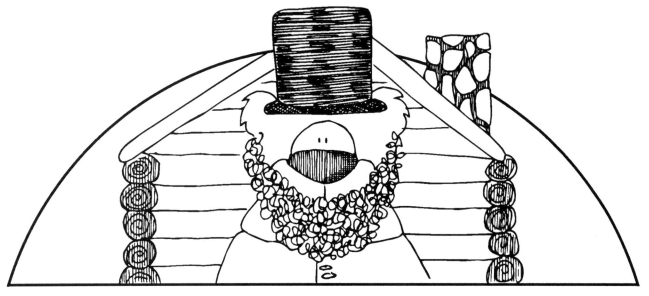

Birthday: February 12, 1809

Abraham Lincoln

Abraham Lincoln was born in Kentucky in a humble log cabin. His family was very poor, so young Abe often had to help out on the farm instead of going to school. But by studying on his own and working hard, he rose to become the President of our country at the time of the Civil War. Abraham Lincoln believed that all people should have equal rights, and today he is remembered as the President who gave the slaves their freedom.

Penny Pictures

For each child attach several Lincoln pennies to a tabletop, using small loops of masking tape rolled sticky sides out. Have the children place sheets of white paper on top of their pennies and rub across them with brown crayons. Encourage the children to fill their papers with rubbings and to try overlapping some of their penny pictures to create interesting designs.

Extension: If desired, cover the children's decorated papers with clear self-stick paper to make placemats for snacktime.

Log Cabin Mural

Lay brown paper lunch bags out flat and cut off the bottom flaps. Roll up each bag lengthwise and tape along the edges to make "logs." Place a sheet of butcher paper on a table or on the floor. Then let the children work together to glue the logs on the butcher paper in a log cabin shape. When they have finished, add a construction paper chimney and several green tree shapes, if desired. Display the mural on a wall or a bulletin board.

Variation: Use any size of brown paper bags to make the logs and cut them to a uniform length.

Storytime Fun

Select a variety of familiar picture books to set out at storytime. Talk with the children about how young Abe Lincoln liked to stay up late at night reading by the light of the fire. Explain that he said he loved books because he could always learn new things from them. Encourage the children to tell about their favorite books or stories. Can they find picture books among those you set out that have helped them to learn new things? Let the children choose one of the books they think that young Abraham Lincoln might have liked. Then read the book aloud for Abe on his birthday.

Abraham Lincoln

Under Lincoln's Hat

For this activity you will need a black top hat (or an oatmeal box decorated to look like one) and five or six small toys or other objects. Have the children sit with you in a circle. Place the objects in the middle of the circle and have the children name each one. Then have the children close their eyes as you hide one of the objects under the hat. When the children open their eyes, have them try guessing which object is under Lincoln's hat. Let the child who first guesses correctly hide a different object under the hat for the next round of the game. Continue until each child has had a chance to hide an object.

Log Cabin Board Game

On a piece of posterboard trace around a tongue depressor to create a cabin made of six logs (see illustration). Number the logs as indicated from 1 to 6. Select six tongue depressors and number them from 1 to 6 by drawing on sets of dots. Then let the children take turns placing the tongue depressors on top of the matching numbered logs on the gameboard.

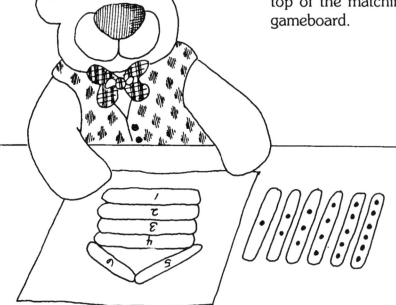

Lincoln Penny Toss

Decorate an oatmeal box to resemble a black top hat. Place the hat upside down on the floor. Then let the children stand a few feet away from the hat and take turns tossing pennies into it. After each round of the game, remove the pennies from the hat and count them with the children.

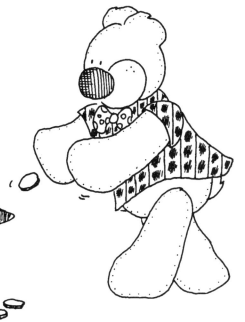

Lincoln Was Our President

Sung to: "Pop! Goes the Weasel"

Abraham Lincoln was a man
Who set the people free.
He wore a tall hat and had a dark beard,
Our President was he.
All around the country,
The people were at war.
Lincoln helped to save our land
And so much more.

Barbara Paxson

Log Cabin Snacks

Give each child some peanut butter and several square wheat crackers on a small plate. Let the children use plastic knives to spread the peanut butter on their crackers. Then let them stack their crackers to create "log cabins."

Abraham Lincoln

Birthday: February 22, 1732

George Washington

George Washington is remembered as the "Father of Our Country." He was born on a plantation in Virginia at the time when America still belonged to England. When he grew up, he became Commander in Chief of the American army and led his troops to victory in the War of Independence. Later, he helped form our nation's government and was elected to be our first President.

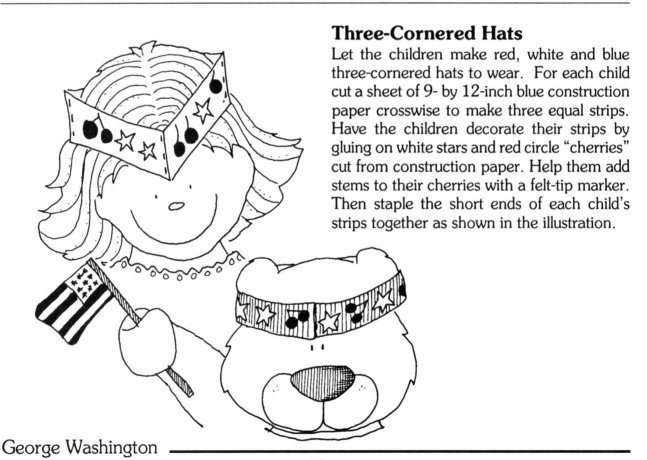

Three-Cornered Hats

Let the children make red, white and blue three-cornered hats to wear. For each child cut a sheet of 9- by 12-inch blue construction paper crosswise to make three equal strips. Have the children decorate their strips by gluing on white stars and red circle "cherries" cut from construction paper. Help them add stems to their cherries with a felt-tip marker. Then staple the short ends of each child's strips together as shown in the illustration.

George Washington

Washington Cherry Trees

For each child glue or tape a twig "tree" to a sheet of white construction paper. Give the children red self-stick dots to use for cherries. Then let them attach the dots to their papers, some as if growing on their tree branches and some as if falling off.

Variation: Instead of using self-stick dots, let the children glue on circles punched with a hole punch from red construction paper.

George Washington and the Cherry Tree

At storytime tell the following legend about George Washington and the cherry tree: "When George Washington was a boy, his father planted a small cherry tree in the garden. Soon there were ripe red cherries growing on its branches. One day when George was out playing in the garden, he chopped down the cherry tree with his little hatchet. Later, his father saw the tree and demanded to know who had cut it down. George knew that he had been very naughty and that his father was angry. But he said bravely, 'I cannot tell a lie, Father. It was I.'" Talk with the children about the story. How do they think George felt after chopping down the cherry tree? What do they think his father might have done when he heard what George said? How does this story help us to know that George Washington was brave and honest?

Extension: Let the children take turns playing the roles of George and his father and acting out the story.

George Washington

Washington Cherry Count

Make a felt tree and ten felt cherries and place the tree on a flannelboard. Use a felt-tip marker to number the cherries from 1 to 10. Let each child in turn choose a cherry, identify the number on it and place the cherry on the tree. When all the cherries are on the tree, count them together with the children.

Crossing the Delaware

Let the children play a game of "Washington Crossing the Delaware." Place two pieces of blue yarn several feet apart on the floor for a river. Then let the children take turns tossing a Washington quarter across the river into a box or other container. Continue the game until each child has succeeded in tossing the quarter into the container at least once.

Hint: Make the river wider or narrower depending on the ages and abilities of the children.

George Washington

Fife and Drum Parade

Have the children put on their three-cornered hats from the activity on p. 62 and line up for a parade. Let several children at a time lead the parade, playing drums and tootling through plastic straw "fifes." As the children march around the room, have them sing "Yankee Doodle" or the song on this page.

George Washington

Sung to: "Yankee Doodle"

George Washington was the first
President of our country.
The people loved him, one and all,
He worked to make our land free.
He led the soldiers — that was hard,
For they were cold and hungry.
He said, "Be brave, now don't give up.
We'll build a brand new country."

Vicki Claybrook

Cherry Yogurt Snacks

Spoon cherry yogurt into small bowls. Let each child top his or her serving with a sprinkling of nut-like cereal and a red cherry. Serve with cups of cherry-flavored seltzer, if desired.

Birthday: March 3, 1847

Alexander Graham Bell

In 1876 Alexander Graham Bell was working on a machine to aid the deaf when he invented the telephone. His invention was a great success, and soon there were telephones all over the world. For the first time, people did not have to meet in order to have conversations. Thanks to Alexander Graham Bell, they could speak with one another no matter how far apart they lived.

Telephone Wire Art

Purchase telephone cord wire at a hardware store. Slit open the outer covering of the cord and remove the thin strands of colored wire that are inside. Cut the wires into short pieces and let the children have fun twisting them into free-form shapes. Then hang the shapes as mobiles or string them on yarn to make necklaces.

Alexander Graham Bell

Using a Telephone

Bring in a touch-button telephone. Without plugging it in, use the phone for doing the activities below.

- Point out the numbers on the phone buttons and read through them with the children. Demonstrate how to dial telephone numbers by pushing the buttons. Then help each child in turn dial his or her home telephone number.

- Let the children take turns dialing one another's home phone numbers. Have the children dictate their own numbers or dictate them yourself.

- Set out a second real or toy telephone. Then "call up" each child in turn and have a short conversation. Use this opportunity to help the children learn appropriate ways of speaking on the phone.

- Discuss the 911 emergency number and the kinds of situations in which it is appropriate to call it. Then let each child have a chance to practice dialing the number and reporting an "emergency."

Calling Home

Arrange ahead of time for each child to call his or her own telephone number and speak to someone who is at home. Give each child an index card with his or her telephone number written on it. Encourage the children to try memorizing their numbers by tracing over them with their fingers while saying them out loud. Then help the children make their calls on a working telephone.

Alexander Graham Bell

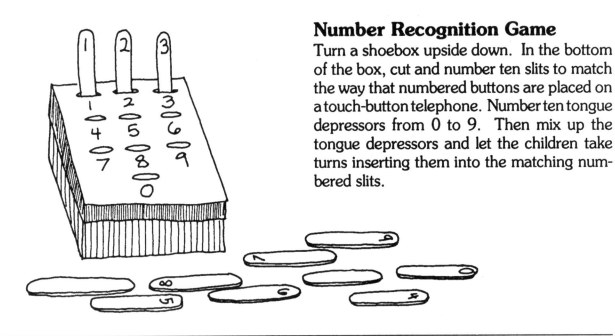

Number Recognition Game

Turn a shoebox upside down. In the bottom of the box, cut and number ten slits to match the way that numbered buttons are placed on a touch-button telephone. Number ten tongue depressors from 0 to 9. Then mix up the tongue depressors and let the children take turns inserting them into the matching numbered slits.

Learning Telephone Numbers

Write each child's home telephone number on an index card. Have the children sit with you in a circle. Then sing the song below for each child while holding up the card with his or her telehone number on it.

Sung to: "Ten Little Indians"

Let's call Lisa on the phone,
Let's call Lisa on the phone,
Let's call Lisa on the phone.
Let's call her right now.

Five-five-five, one-two-three-four,
Five-five-five, one-two-three-four,
Five-five-five, one-two-three-four.
Let's call Lisa now.

Elizabeth McKinnon

Alexander Graham Bell

Telephone Trivia

For this game you will need a toy telephone, a bell and small prizes (stickers, paper flower shapes, etc.). Have the children sit in a circle. Let them pass the toy telephone around the circle until you ring the bell. Have the child holding the phone lift up the receiver and say, "Hello, this is (child's name)." Ask the child a trivia question such as "What color is Rudolph's nose?" or "What animal is green, hops and says 'ribbit?'" Keep giving clues until the child answers correctly. Then let the child choose a prize. Continue the game until every child has received a phone call.

Alexander Graham Bell

Sung to: "Frere Jacques"

Alexander, Alexander
Graham Bell, Graham Bell.
He made something useful,
He made something useful.
Ring, ring, ring; ring, ring, ring.

Let the children sing the song and then tell what Alexander Graham Bell invented.

Saundra Winnett

Snacktime Fun

At snacktime make mini pizzas by placing tomato sauce and grated cheese on toasted English muffin halves. Prepare several other kinds of toppings such as cooked sausage, mushrooms and olives. Then let each child in turn call you on a toy telephone and place an order for the kind of pizza he or she wants. Add the desired toppings to the children's pizzas, place them on a cookie sheet and broil them until the cheese is hot and bubbly. If desired, deliver the warm pizzas to the snack table in a real pizza box.

Birthday: March 14, 1864

Casey Jones

Casey Jones was a fine railroad engineer. Whenever his train came roaring down the track, everyone knew that it was sure to make the next station on time. After giving his life to save his passengers in a train wreck, Casey Jones became a popular folk hero. The story of his brave deed lives on today in American folk music.

Egg Carton Trains
Give each child a row of six egg cups cut from a cardboard egg carton and half of a cardboard toilet tissue tube. Have the children turn their egg cup rows upside down and paint them as desired to create trains. Then have them paint their cardboard tubes black to make smokestacks. When the paint has dried, help the children glue their smokestacks to the tops of the first cups on their egg carton trains.

Cardboard Carton Train Cars

Give each child a cardboard carton (large enough to sit in) with the top and bottom removed. Provide the children with felt-tip markers and let them decorate the sides of their cartons to look like train cars. Make a set of suspenders for each carton by attaching two pieces of heavy yarn from front to back. Have the children get inside their train cars and help them hang their suspenders over their shoulders. Then let them chug around the room as one long train.

Extension: Let the children line up their train cars on the floor and place dolls or stuffed animals inside for passengers.

Choo-Choo Train

Talk with the children about the different kinds of things that trains carry from place to place. Then recite the poem below and let the children take turns filling in the blanks.

The train goes chugging up and down,
Carrying _____ from town to town.
It carries _____ and _____ too,
And as it goes, it says "Choo-choo!"

Elizabeth McKinnon

Color Train

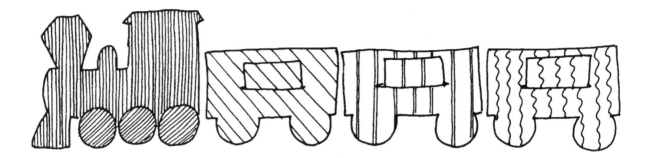

Cut a train engine shape out of black construction paper and one boxcar shape each out of red, yellow, blue, green, orange, purple and brown construction paper. Make a "box" for each boxcar by cutting out a matching colored square. Cut slits in the boxcars to hold the boxes. Then let the children take turns lining up the boxcars behind the engine and inserting the boxes in the slits of the matching colored boxcars.

Sorting Train

Make a train by stringing together several small open boxes. If desired, cut wheels from posterboard and attach them to the boxes with brass paper fasteners. Let the children use the train for sorting different geometric shapes cut from construction paper, different pasta shapes or different colored buttons.

Casey Jones Song

Sung to: "Frere Jacques"

Casey Jones, Casey Jones,
Clickety-clack, clickety-clack.
See his train a-chugging,
Chug-a-chug-a-chugging,
Down the track, down the track.

Casey Jones, Casey Jones,
Clickety-clack, clickety-clack.
See his engine puffing,
Puff-a-puff-a-puffing,
Down the track, down the track.

Casey Jones, Casey Jones,
Clickety-clack, clickety-clack.
Hear his whistle tooting,
Toot-a-toot-a-tooting,
Down the track, down the track.

Elizabeth McKinnon

Casey Jones

Little Red Train

Have the children pretend to be train cars lined up in a row at the station. Chug around the room as everyone sings the song below. Each time you pass by the station, have the child at the head of the line hook onto the back of your train. Continue until everyone is hooked on and has had a chance to chug around the room.

Sung to: "Row, Row, Row Your Boat"

Here comes the Little Red Train,
Chugging down the track.
It first goes down, then turns around,
Then it chugs right back.

See it hook on cars,
Chugging as it goes.
The Little Red Train never stops,
It just grows and grows.

Jean Warren

Railroad Dining

Have the children line up their cardboard carton train cars from the activity on p. 71. Set out bowls of finger snacks such as pretzels, cheese cubes, carrot sticks and apple slices. Let each child place items from the bowls into a recloseable plastic sandwich bag. Help the children seal their bags. Then let them climb inside their cardboard cartons and enjoy eating their snacks on their train.

Birthday: March 24, 1874

Harry Houdini

Harry Houdini was a great magician. Born Erich Weiss, he started out performing magic acts with his brother in small clubs, where they were billed as the Brothers Houdini. He became a superstar when he teamed up with his wife, Bess, and created the incredible escape tricks that brought him world-wide fame.

Magic Pictures

For each child draw a picture on a piece of white construction paper with a white crayon. (Be sure to press down hard with the crayon while you are drawing.) Set out brushes and dark colors of thinned tempera paint. Then let the children brush the paint over their papers and watch as the white crayon pictures appear like magic.

Hocus-Pocus

Make a "magic wand" by stapling a star cut from construction paper to the end of a plastic straw. Decorate the star with glitter, if desired. Ask the children to form a circle. Choose one child to be the Magician and give him or her the magic wand. Have the Magician stand in the middle of the circle, wave the magic wand and say: "Hocus-Pocus, Ala-Kazaam. Turn into (dogs/pigs/etc.) if you can." Have the other children move around the room pretending to be the animal named. Then have the Magician wave the magic wand again and call out the words that will change the animals back into children: "Hocus-Pocus, Ala-Kazoo. Now turn back into you." Continue the game until every child has had a turn being the Magician.

Variation: Make a magic wand for each child to decorate as desired. Then let the children take turns waving their wands and describing the "magic" they are making happen.

Rabbits From a Hat

Cut ten rabbit shapes out of white posterboard and place them in a black top hat (or any kind of similar hat). Have the children sit with you in a circle. Begin by placing the hat in front of one child and announcing, "Ladies and gentlemen, the great Houdini will now pull (two/five/etc.) rabbits out of a hat." Have the child take out the designated number of rabbits, one at a time, and hold them up as everyone counts. Then have the child put all the rabbits back into the hat. Continue the game until everyone has had a turn.

Harry Houdini

Help Houdini Escape

Line up three paper cups on a table. Place a button under one cup to represent Houdini. Move the cups around as the children watch. Then let them take turns guessing which cup Houdini is under and lifting the cups to see if their guesses were correct. Let the child who first "helps Houdini escape" place the button under a cup for the next round of the game. Continue until each child has had a turn placing the button under a cup.

Water Magic

Let the children have fun doing this "magic" science experiment. Float corks in a tub of water and set out clear plastic cups. Ask the children to try using the cups to make the corks sink without touching them with their hands or cups. Then show them how to place a cup upside down over a cork and push the cup into the water. (The cork will appear to sink because the compressed air in the cup pushes the water level down.) Let the children try experimenting again.

Magic Tricks

Try doing the magic tricks below with the children.

*   Stand sideways to a wall with your right foot and right shoulder pressed up against it. Then try lifting your left leg. (You can't do it because leaning against the wall changes your center of gravity.)

*   Hold a penny between your two ring fingers while pressing the knuckles of both hands tightly together. Then try dropping the penny. (You can't do it because your ring fingers cannot move independently of your other fingers.)

Harry Houdini

The Great Houdini
Sung to: "The Mulberry Bush"

The great Houdini did magic acts,
Magic acts, magic acts.
The great Houdini did magic acts,
Let's do some, too, today.

Abracadabra! We're rockets now,
Rockets now, rockets now.
Abracadabra! We're rockets now,
Let's zoom around this way.

Additional verses: "Abracadabra! We're wiggle worms
now/Let's wiggle around this way; Abracadabra! We're
windmills now/Let's move our arms this way," etc.
Encourage the children to come up with their own ideas
for similar verses.

Elizabeth McKinnon

Magic Muffins
For snacktime make these "magic muffins"
that have sweet surprises hidden inside. Sift
together into a large bowl 1 cup white flour, 1
tablespoon baking powder and $\frac{1}{2}$ teaspoon
salt. Stir in $\frac{3}{4}$ cup whole-wheat or graham
flour. In a blender process together 1 egg, $\frac{1}{2}$
cup unsweetened frozen apple juice concen-
trate, $\frac{1}{4}$ cup vegetable oil, $\frac{1}{2}$ cup milk and 1
sliced banana. Pour the liquid ingredients into
the dry ingredients and mix well. Generously
grease a 12-cup muffin tin (or use paper
baking cups). Fill the muffin tin cups halfway
with batter. Place a piece of fresh or canned
fruit in each cup, then add more batter. Bake
at 400 degrees for 20 to 25 minutes. Makes
12 muffins.

Harry Houdini

Birthday: April 26, 1785

John J. Audubon

John James Audubon was an artist who is best known for his beautiful bird paintings. He liked to walk through the countryside looking for birds and painting them in their natural surroundings. In the 1830s he published a collection of his lifelike paintings called *Birds of America*, which brought him great fame. The Audubon Society, one of our country's largest conservation agencies, was named after John J. Audubon.

Bird Pictures

Give each child a bird shape cut from white construction paper. Set out feathers and different colors of tempera paints. Let the children use the feathers as brushes to paint their birds any color they wish. When the paint has dried, have the children glue their birds on pieces of light blue construction paper. Let them use felt-tip markers to add eyes, legs, feet and other details. Then help them tape leafy twigs to their papers for their birds to stand on.

John J. Audubon

Audubon Bird Paintings

Check your local library for a copy of *The Birds of America* by John James Audubon. (Or ask a librarian to help you find other resources that contain examples of Audubon's paintings.) Select several of the bird pictures to show to the children. Talk with them about the colors, sizes and shapes of the birds and about what the birds are doing. Encourage the children to compare different pictures. How are the birds and their settings alike? How are they different?

Bird Concentration

Purchase two each of six different bird stickers. Attach one sticker to each of twelve index cards. Spread out the cards face down on a table or on the floor. Let one child begin by turning up two cards. If the birds on the cards match, let the child keep the cards. If the birds don't match, have the child replace both cards face down exactly where they were before. Continue the game until all the cards have been matched. Then let the child who ended up with the most cards have the first turn when you start the game again.

Bird Nest Game

Let each child make a bird nest by arranging grass, twigs, leaves and pieces of string in the bottom of a margarine tub. Give each child five cotton balls to use for eggs. Number five index cards from 1 to 5. Hold up a card and ask the children to identify the number on it. Then have them place that number of eggs in their bird nests. Have them remove the eggs before you hold up the next card. Continue until all the cards have been used. When the game is over, let the children replace all their eggs and display their bird nests around the room.

John J. Audubon

Bird Watching

Take the children on a bird-watching walk through your neighborhood. Along the way, ask them to look for birds of different sizes and colors and to listen for the sounds that the birds make. Point out familiar birds, such as robins or pigeons, and have the children observe how the birds fly, how they sit when they rest and how they walk around looking for food. When you return to your room, let each child tell something about a bird that he or she saw.

Extension: If desired, make binoculars for the children to take with them when they go bird watching. For each child tape two cardboard toilet tissue tubes together side by side. Then attach a long piece of string or yarn for a neck strap.

Flying Fast, Flying Slow

Make a pair of wings for each child by taping colored crepe paper strips to a long piece of yarn. Safety-pin the center of the yarn to the back of the child's shirt neckband and tie the ends of the yarn around the child's wrists. Then recite the poem below with the children and let them "fly" around the room.

Flying fast, flying slow,
Flying high, flying low.
Swooping and swirling,
I glide through the air.
My bird wings take me everywhere!

Jean Warren

John J. Audubon

80

Like Audubon Did

Sung to: "Did You Ever See a Lassie"

Oh, let's paint a pretty red bird,
A red bird, a red bird,
Oh, let's paint a pretty red bird
Like Audubon did.
A red bird, a red bird,
A red bird, a red bird,
Oh, let's paint a pretty red bird
Like Audubon did.

Hold up bird shapes cut from different colors of construction paper and sing a verse of the song for each color. Let the children pretend to hold brushes and make painting movements as they sing.

Elizabeth McKinnon

Seed Treats

Let the children make seed treats to eat for snacktime. Have them spread softened cream cheese or peanut butter on crackers. Then let them sprinkle on sunflower or sesame seeds.

Extension: When the children have finished eating their snacks, let them scatter their leftover crumbs and seeds outside for the birds to enjoy.

John J. Audubon

Birthday: May 5, 1867

Nellie Bly

Nellie Bly was a newspaper reporter whose real name was Elizabeth Cochrane. She became famous in 1889 when she went around in the world in seventy-two days, beating the record set in Jules Verne's popular novel *Around the World in Eighty Days*. Traveling by ship, train, handcart and donkey, she wrote stories and cabled them back to her newspaper so that people at home could follow her route and read her latest news.

Newspaper Collages

Give each child a sheet of black construction paper. Set out glue and squares of newspaper. Have the children tear the newspaper squares into different sized pieces. Then have them glue the pieces on their papers to create collages. While the glue is still wet, let the children sprinkle on silver glitter, if desired.

Nellie Bly

What's In the Newspaper?

Look through a newspaper and mark appropriate items to read to the children. Have the children sit with you in a circle. Then hold the newspaper so that they can see it and read the marked items to them. Talk about how the news items are written by reporters, who often go to where the news is happening so they can write about it firsthand.

News of the Day

Let the children take turns reporting some news about themselves. For example, did anyone visit a special place recently or get a new pet or new clothes? Write the children's responses on large sheets of newsprint to make a group newspaper. Title the paper "News of the Day" (or let the children make up their own newspaper name). Display the newspaper pages on a wall at the children's eye level and arrange a time for a group "reading."

Nellie Bly

Traveling to Old Bombay

Ask the children to imagine that they are going on a trip around the world to visit old Bombay. Then read the open-ended poem below and let them fill in the blanks.

Ready, set, go! We're on our way,
Off to visit old Bombay.

First we'll ride on a _____ going our way,
As we travel to old Bombay.

Next we'll catch a _____ going our way,
On our journey to old Bombay.

Then we'll hop aboard a _____ going our way,
As we travel to old Bombay.

Finally we'll jump on a _____ going our way,
On our journey to old Bombay.

Here we are at last in old Bombay. Traveling can be fun if you know your way!

Jean Warren

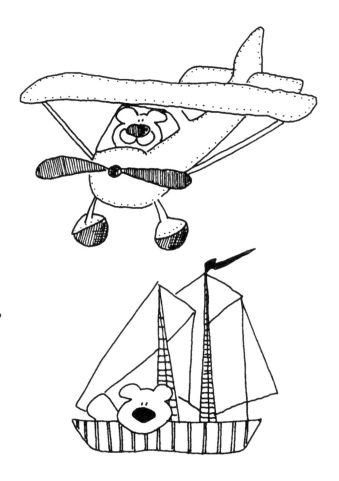

By Land, Sea or Air

Today, we have many more ways of traveling than Nellie Bly did when she went around the world. Cut out pictures of vehicles that travel on land, vehicles that travel on water and vehicles that travel in air. Mount the pictures on heavy paper and mix them up. Then let the children sort the pictures into three piles according to where the vehicles travel.

Around the World

Make a gameboard by drawing a large dough-nut shape on a piece of posterboard and dividing it into six sections. Write the numerals 1 to 6 in the sections in random order. Give one child a small plastic figure to represent Nellie Bly. Have the child move the figure around the numbered sections on the gameboard as everyone chants: "Around and around the world Nellie goes. Where she will stop, nobody knows." At the end of the chant, have the child stop moving the figure and identify the number on which Nellie is standing. Continue the game until everyone has had a turn.

Variation: Label the sections of the gameboard with different colors or geometric shapes.

Around-the-World Snacks

At snacktime set out foods that represent places from around the world, such as French bread slices, Swiss cheese cubes, Mexican tortilla chips, Chinese noodles and Hawaiian pineapple chunks. Let the children choose small amounts of the different foods to place on plates for tasting.

Hint: Use rectangles cut from newspaper for placemats.

Nellie Bly Went Around the World
Sung to: "The Wheels on the Bus"

Oh, Nellie Bly went around the world,
Around the world, around the world.
Oh, Nellie Bly went around the world,
Many years ago.

She sailed in a ship as around she went,
Around she went, around she went.
She sailed in a ship as around she went,
Many years ago.

Additional verses: "She chugged in a train as around she went; She traveled in a cart as around she went; She bounced on a donkey as around she went; She wrote news stories as around she went."

Elizabeth McKinnon

Nellie Bly

Birthday: June 8, 1867

Frank Lloyd Wright

Frank Lloyd Wright was a great architect who changed the American idea of what a home could be. In his time, most houses had rooms that were closed off by walls and doors. He became famous for designing homes with open rooms and plate glass windows that allowed indoor and outdoor spaces to flow together.

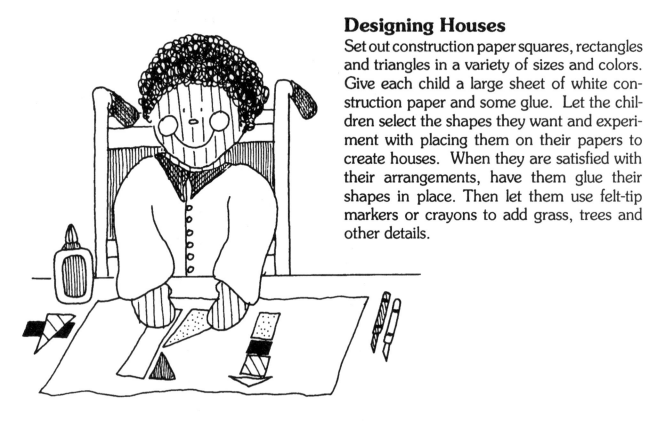

Designing Houses

Set out construction paper squares, rectangles and triangles in a variety of sizes and colors. Give each child a large sheet of white construction paper and some glue. Let the children select the shapes they want and experiment with placing them on their papers to create houses. When they are satisfied with their arrangements, have them glue their shapes in place. Then let them use felt-tip markers or crayons to add grass, trees and other details.

Making a Dollhouse

Let the children help make a dollhouse to use for dramatic play. Use shoeboxes with the lids removed for individual rooms. Turn the boxes on their sides and stack them as desired, fastening them together with tape or glue. Decorate the walls with wallpaper cut from sample books and attach construction paper "carpets" to the floors. Cut pictures of furniture and people out of store catalogs. Glue the pictures to empty thread spools to help them stand properly. Then let the children have fun arranging the furniture in the different rooms and playing house with their dollhouse people.

Where Do We Live?

Have the children sit with you in a circle. Ask them to tell where they live (in a house, an apartment, a mobile home, etc.). Then recite the poem below for each child.

A squirrel lives in a tree,
  (Tent fingers to make tree shape.)
A snail lives in a shell.
  (Cover fist with opposite hand.)
A bear lives in a cave,
  (Make fist with thumb inside.)
It suits her very well.

A fish lives in a fishbowl,
  (Make circle with hands.)
A bird lives in a nest.
  (Cup hands together.)
Matthew lives in a house,
  (Make roof above head with arms.)
He thinks his home is best.

Elizabeth McKinnon

Frank Lloyd Wright

House Shapes Games

Cut one small, one medium and one large house shape each from red, yellow and blue posterboard. Set out the shapes and let the children use them for the following games:

- Sort the houses by size and by color.

- Count the houses by size and by color. Place one red house next to two blue houses and count how many there are all together, etc.

- Line up the houses from smallest to largest by color, then all together.

- Line up the houses in various patterns by color and by size.

House Floor Plan

On a large piece of paper, draw and label a house floor plan that includes a living room, a bedroom, a kitchen and a bathroom. Cut pictures from magazines of furniture, fixtures and appliances that would be found in each of the four rooms. Mount the pictures on heavy paper and trim around the edges. Place all of the pictures in a box. Then let the children take turns choosing pictures from the box, naming the items and placing them in the appropriate rooms on the floor plan.

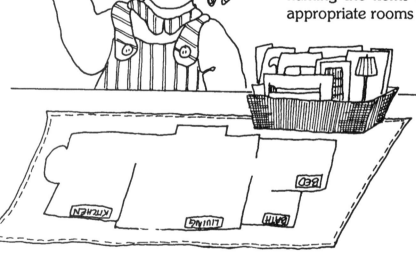

Frank Lloyd Wright

Block House

Select blocks of different sizes and shapes and place them in a box. Have the children sit in a circle. Let one child begin by taking a block from the box and placing it in the middle of the circle. Then let the other children take turns choosing blocks and adding them to the first one to create a house. Continue in the same manner until all the blocks have been used or until the children feel that their block house is completed.

Frank Lloyd Wright
Sung to: "Three Blind Mice"

Frank Lloyd Wright, Frank Lloyd Wright,
He liked to draw, he liked to plan.
He drew new houses so open and wide,
He brought the outdoors right inside,
His plans for houses became our guide.
Frank Lloyd Wright.

Jean Warren

Mini House Sandwiches

Let the children help make mini house sandwiches for snacktime. For four sandwiches, cut the crusts off two slices of bread and spread on peanut butter. Cut one slice into four squares and the other slice into four triangles. Have the children arrange the bread squares on their plates. Then have them place a bread triangle above each square for a roof. Let them decorate their mini houses with sunflower seeds, raisins or shredded coconut, if desired.

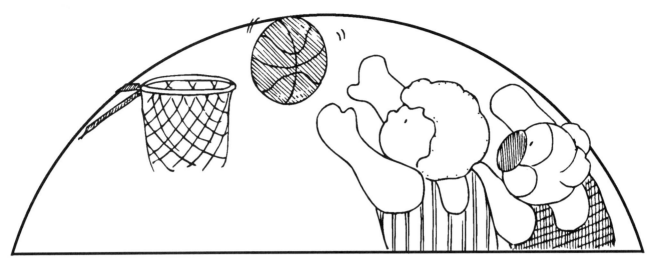

Birthday: June 16, 1911

Babe Didrikson

Babe Didrikson loved all sports. From the time she was a girl, she devoted herself to athletics and constantly worked to improve her skills. Not only was she an Olympic winner in track and field, she also excelled in basketball, baseball, tennis and swimming. In her later years, she won fame as an outstanding golf player. Born Mildred Ella, Babe got her nickname from the famous baseball player Babe Ruth.

Good Sports Mural

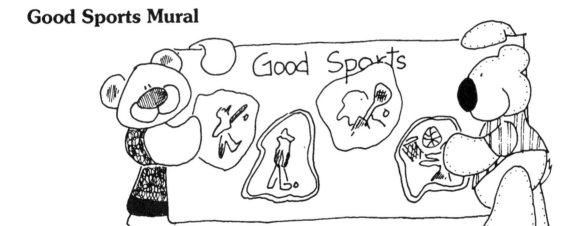

Set out magazines or store catalogs that deal with sports and fitness. Let the children look through them and tear out pictures of people doing different kinds of sports and exercise activities. Have the children glue their pictures on a piece of butcher paper. Write "Good Sports" at the top of the paper and hang the mural on a wall at the children's eye level. Then talk with the children about the different kinds of activities that are shown in the pictures.

Variation: Let younger children choose from precut pictures that have been placed in a box.

Sports Charades

Have the children sit together in a group. Whisper in one child's ear the name of a sport (basketball, golf, swimming, baseball, skating, bowling, etc.). Then let the child stand in front of the group and act out the sport while the other children try guessing what it is. Continue until everyone has had a turn.

Exercise Time

Number ten index cards from 1 to 10. Hold the cards in your hand and have the children stand around you in a large circle. Let one child draw a card from your hand and identify the number on it. Then name an exercise and have all the children do it that number of times. For example, if the number 6 card was chosen, have the children touch their toes six times or do six jumping jacks. Continue until each child has had a chance to draw a card.

Variation: Let the child who draws a card name the exercise to be performed.

Ball Games

Set out different kinds and sizes of balls and let the children enjoy the games below. Encourage them to make up their own games as well.

- Sort the balls by kind.

- Line up the balls from smallest to largest.

- Bounce a ball a designated number of times.

- Bounce a ball back and forth with a partner.

- Make "baskets" by tossing a beach ball into a wastebasket or other container.

- Play "golf" using long cardboard tubes and plastic golf balls.

- Roll a ball down a hallway to knock over milk carton "bowling pins."

Relay Race

Have the children line up in rows of five or six. Give the first child in each row a beanbag. Have the children pass the beanbags over their heads to the children behind them. When the last children in the rows are passed the beanbags, have them move to the fronts of the lines. Continue until each child has had a turn being first in line. As the rows finish, have the children sit down and cheer for the groups still playing until all the rows are done.

Variation: Instead of passing beanbags over their heads, have the children try these other relays: passing beanbags between their legs; skipping across the room, then hopping back; carrying a cotton ball on a spoon to a table, then walking back.

Babe Didrikson

Obstacle Course

Set up an obstacle course in your room. Include such things for the children to do as walking on a balance beam, crawling through a tunnel or under a table, jumping over single blocks (do not stack them), climbing up and down stairs and walking a crooked line taped to the floor. Let the children go through the obstacle course at their own pace. Speed is not important.

Babe Didrikson

Sung to: "Three Blind Mice"

Babe Didrikson, Babe Didrikson,
She loved sports, she loved sports.
She loved to play ball and she loved to run,
She thought that swimming and tennis were
   fun,
At playing golf she was Number One.
Babe Didrikson.

Elizabeth McKinnon

High-Energy Shakes

Let the children enjoy these nutritious drinks at snacktime. In a blender container combine one 6-ounce can unsweetened frozen orange juice concentrate, $1/3$ cup nonfat dry milk, 1 cup water and $1/2$ cup crushed ice. Blend until smooth and frothy. Makes 5 small servings.

Birthday: June 27, 1880

Helen Keller

Helen Keller was just a baby when she lost her sight and hearing. With the help of her teacher, Annie Sullivan, she learned how to use her other senses to explore her world and communicate with other people. She grew up to become famous for her achievements in writing and lecturing and for leading a life dedicated to inspiring and helping others.

Sensory Art

Let the children fingerpaint on pieces of butcher paper with scented shaving cream. Talk with them about how the shaving cream smells and feels. Sprinkle a little cornmeal on the children's papers and ask them to describe the new texture they feel. Then sprinkle on small amounts of powder tempera paint. As the children continue fingerpainting, encourage them to talk about what their designs look like.

Variation: Let the children create with different colors of playdough that have been scented with drops of peppermint, lemon or vanilla extract. If desired, mix sand with some of the playdough to create a different texture.

Helen Keller

Using the Five Senses

Do this activity in a circle with several children at a time. Pass around an orange for the children to examine. Ask them to describe how it looks. Have them close their eyes as you pass the orange around again. Ask them to tell how the orange feels as they hold and touch it. Have them listen carefully as you peel the orange. Can they describe the sound they hear? Then divide up the orange and give each of the children a segment. Have them close their eyes again and describe how the orange smells, then how it tastes.

Look and Match

Make sets of "before" and "after" bags. For each set, you will need two recloseable plastic sandwich bags and the same item in two different forms (whole crackers and cracker crumbs, crayons and crayon shavings, colored paper and confetti, rocks and sand, etc.). Put one form of the item in each bag and make as many sets as desired. Mix up the bags and place them on a table. Then let the children take turns examining the contents and matching the "before" bags with the appropriate "after" bags.

Helen Keller

Touch and Tell

Have the children sit with you in a circle. Place several toys or other familiar items in the middle of the circle and ask the children to name them. Put all the items into a large box. Then let the children take turns closing their eyes and taking out items to identify by touch.

Listen and Match

Place objects such as keys, a bell, a drum and a piece of paper in front of a small partition and matching objects behind it. Sit behind the partition and make a sound with one of the objects. Ask a child to find the object in front of the partition that makes the same sound.

Sniff and Tell

Place items with familiar scents in small plastic containers. For example, you might use peanut butter, baby powder, an orange peel and a flower. Cover each container with foil and punch a few tiny holes in the top. Then let the children take turns sniffing the containers and identifying the source of each scent.

Helen Keller

Helen Keller's Birthday Song

Teach the children how to sign the words "Happy birthday to you" as shown in the illustrations. Then sing the song below.

Happy
Tap chest with palm, bring up and forward twice.

Birth-
Right hand, palm facing chest, moves forward and is placed in palm of left hand.

day
Right hand moves across body.

To
Right index finger moves towards left index finger.

You
Right index finger points at a particular person or a space where a person might be.

Sung to: "The Muffin Man"

It's Helen Keller's birthday today,
Birthday today, birthday today.
It's Helen Keller's birthday today,
Let's sing and sign this way:

Continue by singing the song "Happy Birthday" and having the children sign the words. Sing the third line of the song as follows: "Happy birthday, happy birthday."

Elizabeth McKinnon

Taste and Compare

At snacktime, set out different forms of the same foods for the children to taste and compare. For example, use grapes and raisins, cucumbers and pickles, scrambled eggs and hard-boiled eggs, and raw apples and apple juice.

Variation: Let the children compare the tastes of different varieties of the same foods. Some examples would be red and green seedless grapes, cheddar and mozzarella cheeses, and sesame and wheat crackers.

Helen Keller

Birthday: July 4, 1776

U.S.A. Each year we celebrate our country's birthday on the Fourth of July, or Independence Day. It was on this day in 1776 that the Declaration of Independence was signed at Philadelphia. Today, we observe Independence Day much like people did long ago by ringing bells, flying flags, joining in parades and setting off fireworks.

Stars and Stripes Collages

Give each child a 9- by 12-inch sheet of blue construction paper. Cut a number of 1- by 9-inch "stripes" out of red and white construction paper. Set out glue and silver star stickers. Then let the children glue the stripes on their papers and attach the stars any way they wish to create their own "stars and stripes" designs.

Variation: Let the children use pieces of red and white plastic tape for stripes.

Fireworks Fun

Give each child a sheet of black construction paper and several different colored pieces of chalk. Help the children draw three or five dots at random on their papers to represent the centers of their fireworks. Have them use one color of chalk to draw short lines radiating out all around each of their dots. Then have them repeat the process using a different color of chalk. Let them continue drawing lines until their colorful bursts of fireworks are almost touching.

Variation: Let the children make fireworks prints by dipping plastic dish scrubbers in tempera paints and lightly pressing them on black construction paper. If desired, tape the papers together and hang them on a wall or a bulletin board to create a sky full of exploding fireworks.

Fourth of July Sorting Game

Cut small, medium and large star shapes and Liberty Bell shapes out of red, white and blue construction paper. Mix up the shapes and place them in a pile. Then let the children take turns sorting the shapes according to color, shape or size.

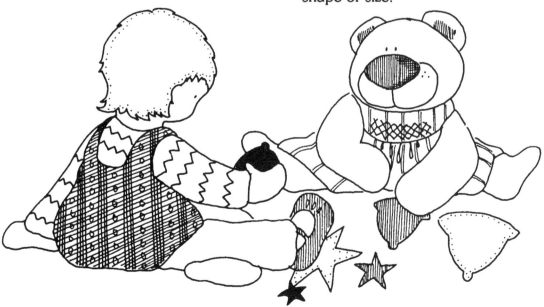

U.S.A.

Flag Time

Hold up an American flag or a picture of one. Talk with the children about how we fly the flag on our country's birthday and encourage them to tell about places they have seen the flag displayed. Ask them to name the colors of the flag. Then as a group, count the red stripes, the white stripes and the stars.

Liberty Bell Ring

Show the children a picture of the Liberty Bell. Explain that the historic bell was rung in 1776 to announce the signing of the Declaration of Independence. Hang a pretend Liberty Bell from the ceiling. Then let the children take turns tossing beanbags or rolled-up socks at the bell to make it ring.

Fourth of July Parade

Let the children enjoy an outdoor Fourth of July Parade to celebrate America's birthday. Have them use red, white and blue crepe paper streamers to decorate bikes, wagons and other riding toys. Hand out several rhythm instruments and small American flags, if desired. Then lead the parade around your yard or neighborhood while singing "Yankee Doodle" and other appropriate songs.

Extension: Make folded newsprint hats for the children to decorate and wear in their parade.

U.S.A.

Fireworks in the Sky
Sung to: "Row, Row, Row Your Boat"

Boom, crack, whistle, pop!
Fireworks in the sky.
See them lighting up the night,
On the Fourth of July!

Red, blue, gold and green,
With fireworks we say,
"Happy Birthday, America,
It's Independence Day!"

Elizabeth McKinnon

Red, White and Blueberries
At snacktime place strawberries and blueberries in separate bowls. Let the children take turns mashing the berries with forks. Give each child some plain yogurt in a small bowl. Then let the children spoon both kinds of mashed berries over their yogurt to make Fourth of July treats.

U.S.A.

101

Birthday: July 5, 1810

P.T. Barnum

When Phineas Taylor Barnum started the Barnum & Bailey Circus, he called it the "Greatest Show on Earth." His three-ring circus traveled from town to town in its own railroad cars. At every stop crowds of people turned out to see the clowns, animals, trapeze artists and acrobats perform under the Big Top. One of Barnum's most famous circus attractions was Jumbo, a giant elephant whose name we still use today to mean "extra large."

Paper Plate Clowns

Give each child a paper plate to use for a clown face. Have the children glue large construction paper triangles to their plates for clown hats. Then give them small construction paper squares, circles and triangles to glue on their plates for facial features. Let the children decorate their clown hats with circle stickers and cotton balls. Let them also glue yarn "hair" on the sides of their plates, if desired.

Extension: Let the children take turns holding their paper plate clowns up to their faces and telling jokes or funny stories.

P.T. Barnum

Circus Elephant Game

Cut elephant shapes ranging from large to small out of gray construction paper. Glue on colorful blankets and headbands cut from construction paper scraps. Write "Jumbo" on the blanket of the largest elephant. If desired, cover the shapes with clear self-stick paper. Then let the children take turns lining up the elephants according to size, with Jumbo at the head of the line and the smallest elephant at the end.

Clown Matching Game

Use a black felt-tip marker to draw an identical clown face and hat on each of ten index cards. Color the hats on each pair of clowns a matching color. Then mix up the cards and let the children take turns finding the clowns with the matching colored hats.

Variation: For a number game, make all the clown hats the same color. Then draw matching numbered sets of black circles on each pair of hats.

Under the Big Top

Collect items that might be seen at a circus (a clown hat, several toy animals, a ball, a balloon, a bag of peanuts, a wire hoop, etc.). Set an opened umbrella on the floor to represent a Big Top and place the circus items underneath it. Have the children sit with you in a semicircle. Start telling a story about going to the circus. Then let the children take turns choosing items from under the Big Top and holding them up. As they do so, incorporate the items into your story. Continue until all the items have been used.

P.T. Barnum

Tightrope Act

Attach a long piece of masking tape to the floor. Have the children line up at one end and take turns "walking the tightrope." If desired, provide a small umbrella for them to hold while they walk the tightrope heel to toe. Then have the children line up again and give them directions such as these: "Walk the tightrope on your toes; Walk the tightrope on your knees; Walk the tightrope using your elbows; Walk the tightrope using your nose."

Circus Train

Let the children work together to make a circus train. Have them decorate cardboard boxes with paints, crepe paper streamers and colorful paper scraps. Hook the boxes together with heavy yarn and add a yarn handle.

Have the children place stuffed animals in the decorated boxes. Then play circus music and let them take turns pulling their circus train around the room.

P.T. Barnum

P.T. Barnum Song
Sung to: "The Mulberry Bush"

Let's march around in a circus parade,
Circus parade, circus parade.
Let's march around in a circus parade
For P.T. Barnum today.

Let's skip like clowns around the ring,
Around the ring, around the ring.
Let's skip like clowns around the ring
For P.T. Barnum today.

Additional verses: "Let's prance like horses around the ring; Let's dance like bears around the ring; Let's stomp like elephants 'round the ring; Let's tiptoe like acrobats 'round the ring," etc.

Elizabeth McKinnon

Circus Snacks
Let the children decorate paper lunch bags with crayon designs. At snacktime place peanuts, pretzels or popcorn inside the bags. Serve with small cups of lemonade, if desired.

Variation: For a special treat, purchase boxes of "Barnum's Animals" animal crackers. Provide one box for each child or divide up the crackers from several boxes and place them in individual sandwich bags. Let the children use the boxes to make a mini circus train.

Birthday: July 30, 1863

Henry Ford

In 1908 Henry Ford pioneered the use of the assembly line to begin mass producing his classic automobile — the Model T. It was the first car ever to be sold at a price the average person could afford, and it was an instant success. During the nineteen years of its production, the Model T was the most popular car on the road.

Then and Now

Show the children a picture of the Model T. Explain that when Henry Ford was making his famous automobile, it was the car most people bought and that it came only in black. Explain also that the Model T had to be started with a hand crank. Then show a picture of a modern automobile and ask the children to compare it with the Model T. How are the cars alike? How are they different?

Henry Ford

Car Collages

Let the children look through magazines and tear or cut out pictures of cars. Then have them glue their pictures on large sheets of construction paper to create car collages. For added fun, give each child a photocopied picture of a Model T to include in his or her collage.

Variation: Let younger children choose from precut pictures placed in a box.

Tire Tracks Art

Cover the art table with newspapers. Pour different colors of tempera paints into shallow containers and set out a number of small plastic cars. Give each child a large piece of construction paper. Then let the children dip the wheels of the cars into the paint and run them back and forth across their papers to create tire tracks.

Variation: Use just two colors of paint (red and yellow, red and blue or blue and yellow). Encourage the children to crisscross their tire tracks and observe the new color created.

Car Puzzles

Cut pictures of cars from magazines, mount them on plain paper and cover them on both sides with clear self-stick paper. Trim around the edges of the pictures and cut each one into several puzzle pieces. Place the pieces of each puzzle in a separate plastic sandwich bag.

Then set out the bags and let the children take turns putting the car puzzles together.

Variation: For a more challenging activity, mix up the pieces from several puzzles and set them out in one pile.

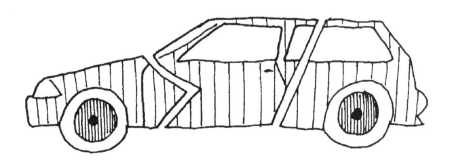

Henry Ford

Parking Garage Game

For this game you will need a large shallow box and a number of different colored toy cars. Place the box upright and cut out a doorway in one side to make a parking garage. On the floor of the garage, draw rectangles that match the colors of the toy cars. Then let the children take turns driving the cars into the garage and parking them on the matching colored "parking stalls."

Variation: To use the parking garage for a number game, write numerals in the parking stalls. Then let the children take turns being the parking garage attendant and telling the drivers which numbered stalls to use for parking their cars.

Road Map

Collect an assortment of toy cars and place them in a box. Use felt-tip markers to draw a map on a large piece of butcher paper. Include roads wide enough for the toy cars to travel on and add trees, houses and other details as desired. Attach the map to the floor with masking tape and place the box of cars nearby. Then let small groups of children have fun driving the cars around on the map.

Variation: To make a permanent map, use a large piece of vinyl material (available at fabric stores) and permanent felt-tip markers.

Henry Ford

Henry Ford Made the Model T

Sung to: "The Wheels on the Bus"

Oh, Henry Ford made the Model T,
Model T, Model T.
Oh, Henry Ford made the Model T,
Many years ago.

The starter on his car went crank-crank-crank,
Crank-crank-crank, crank-crank-crank.
The starter on his car went crank-crank-crank,
Many years ago.

Additional verses: "The engine in his car went putt-putt-putt; The horn on his car went oogah-oo; The top on his car went up and down."

Elizabeth McKinnon

Assembly Line Snacks

Let the children stand at a table and work together in an "assembly line" to help prepare the day's snacks. As a plate is passed down the line, have each child in turn place a different item of food on it (a cracker, a cheese cube, a pickle slice, a carrot round, a celery stick, an apple slice, etc.). Or set out pita pocket halves and let each child in line spoon in a different kind of filling (tuna fish, mayonnaise, shredded lettuce, chopped tomatoes, grated carrots, etc.).

Birthday: August 9, 1944

Smokey Bear

Smokey Bear was created in 1944 as a symbol for the U.S. Forest Service. Wearing his jeans and forest ranger hat, Smokey appears on fire prevention posters, along with his familiar message: "Only You Can Prevent Forest Fires." Since 1950 there has also been a real Smokey Bear living at the National Zoo in Washington, D.C. Among other things, Smokey teaches us that by preventing forest fires we are conserving trees, protecting animal homes and preserving the forests for everyone to enjoy.

Fire Prevention Badges

Cut firefighter badge shapes out of white index cards. Let the children decorate their badges with orange and yellow felt-tip markers. Use a black felt-tip marker to write "(Child's name) does not play with matches" on each child's badge. Then tape a safety pin to the back of the badge and pin it to the child's shirt.

Fire Prevention Posters

Give each child a large sheet of white construction paper and a sprig of evergreen. Set out shallow containers of red, yellow and orange tempera paints. Let the children dip their evergreen sprigs into the paints and brush them across their papers to create flames. When the paint has dried, help the children tape their evergreen sprigs to their papers. Write "Prevent Forest Fires" at the top of each child's paper. Then display the posters on a wall or a bulletin board.

Hi, Smokey

Talk with the children about general fire safety rules: Don't play with matches or lighters; Don't play with electrical cords or sockets; Keep away from things that are hot, etc. Display a picture of Smokey Bear or a Smokey Bear poster. Then let each child have a turn telling Smokey about something that he or she does to help prevent fires.

Note: Smokey Bear posters and other teaching materials may be obtained through your State Forester or your regional office of the U.S. Department of Agriculture Forest Service.

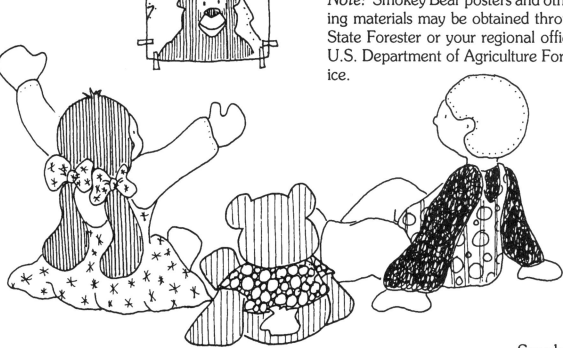

Smokey Bear

The Forest Is Their Home

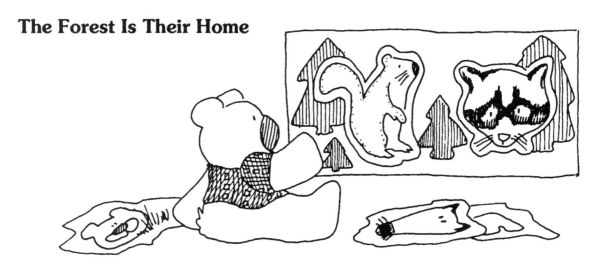

Cut evergreen tree shapes out of felt and arrange them on a flannelboard to create a forest scene. From nature magazines, cut out pictures of different forest animals (a bear, a deer, a fox, a squirrel, etc.). Glue the pictures on heavy paper, trim around the edges and attach felt strips to the backs. Have the children sit with you around the flannelboard and give them each a picture to hold. Then make up a story about the forest and the animals that live there. Each time you introduce an animal into your story, have the child holding that animal picture place it on the flannelboard.

The Forest Gives Us Wood

Discuss with the children how wood from the trees in our forests is used to make houses, furniture, paper products and other items. Then lead the children on a search around the room to see how many different items made from wood they can find.

Extension: Set out several objects that are made from wood (a pencil, a block, a paper cup, etc.) and several objects that are made from other materials (a key, a washcloth, a plastic spoon, etc.). Label one box "Things Made From Wood" and another box "Things Not Made From Wood." Then let the children sort the objects into the appropriate boxes.

Smokey Bear

Plant-A-Forest Game

Paint a shoebox brown and cut six slits in the lid. Number the slits from 1 to 6. Cut six evergreen tree shapes out of green construction paper and attach them to Popsicle sticks. Number the trees from 1 to 6. Then let the children take turns "planting a forest" by inserting the trees in the matching numbered slits in the shoebox lid.

Variation: Number the trees from 1 to 6 by drawing on corresponding sets of brown pinecones.

I Am a Friend of Smokey Bear

Sung to: "Ten Little Indians"

I am a friend of Smokey Bear,
I am a friend of Smokey Bear,
I am a friend of Smokey Bear.
I do what Smokey says.

Smokey says don't play with matches,
Smokey says don't play with matches,
Smokey says don't play with matches.
I do what Smokey says.

Additional verses: "Smokey says don't play with lighters; Smokey says keep away from hot things; Smokey says please protect our forests."

Elizabeth McKinnon

Snacks Along the Trail

Make your own trail mix by combining such foods as dry cereal, raisins, nuts, shredded coconut and dried fruit bits. Spoon the trail mix into recloseable plastic sandwich bags and give one to each child. Then take the children on a pretend forest hike through your neighborhood or a nearby park. Along the way, help the children to appreciate the variety and beauty of the trees they see. When you come to a suitable shady spot, let the children sit down and enjoy eating their trail mix snacks.

Birthdays: August 19, 1871; April 16, 1867

Orville and Wilbur Wright

From the time the Wright Brothers were boys, they dreamed about being able to fly. Their dream came true when they built a glider and added an engine to make the first self-powered airplane. They made their initial flight in their "flying machine" on December 17, 1903, at Kitty Hawk, North Carolina. Today we remember this historic event on Aviation Day, which falls on Orville Wright's birthday.

Making Airplanes

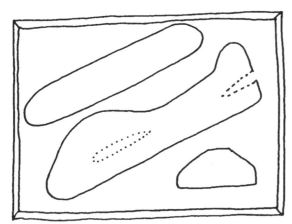

For each child draw an airplane body shape, a wings shape and a tail shape on a Styrofoam food tray (see illustration). Cut out the shapes and make slits in each airplane body as indicated by the dotted lines. Show the children how to insert their wings shapes through the wide slits in their airplane bodies and their tail shapes in the notched slits in the backs. Tape a penny to the nose section of each plane and let the children decorate their airplanes as desired. Then let them have fun flying their planes outside in an open area.

Then and Now

Show the children a picture of the airplane that the Wright Brothers flew at Kitty Hawk. Talk with them about what it might have been like to fly in the plane. Then display pictures or models of modern planes. Ask the children to compare the modern planes to the one the Wright Brothers made. How are the planes similar? How are they different?

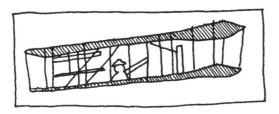

Airplane Stencils

Make airplane-shaped stencils out of light-weight cardboard and use masking tape to attach them to sheets of light blue construction paper. Let the children brush paint over the stencils, using any colors they wish. (The stencils can be used more than once. Just remove them carefully and retape them to clean sheets of paper.) When the paint has dried, let the children glue fluffed-out cotton balls on their papers for clouds, if desired.

Airplane Poem

Recite the poem below and let the children act out the movements.

The airplane has great big wings.
　(Stretch arms out at sides.)
Its propeller spins around and sings.
　(Move one arm around in a circle.)
The airplane goes up — "Vroooom!"
　(Raise arms.)
The airplane goes down — "Vroooom!"
　(Lower arms.)
The airplane flies high
　(Stretch arms out at sides.)
Over our town.
　(Turn around.)

Author Unknown

The Wright Brothers

Sung to: "Pop! Goes the Weasel"

The Wright Brothers made a flying machine.
Can you guess its name?
It had propellers and wings and a tail.
It was an airplane!

Elizabeth McKinnon

Airplane Ticket Game

Line up chairs in rows to represent an airplane cabin. For each child cut one red ticket, one yellow ticket and one blue ticket out of construction paper. Write the child's name on his or her yellow ticket. Mix up the tickets and spread them out on a table. Announce that you are all going to take three airplane rides and that to go on the first ride, everyone must have a red ticket. Have the children walk by the table, pick up red tickets and hand them to you as they board the plane. After they have pretended to fasten their safety belts, walk up and down the aisle talking about how the plane is taking off, how it's now high in the sky, how it's flying over some mountains now, etc. At the end of the trip, have the children get off the plane and pick up blue tickets for the second airplane ride. Then for the third ride back home, have them pick up the yellow tickets that have their names written on them.

Variation: Make tickets that contain different numerals, shapes or alphabet letters.

Orville and Wilbur Wright

Airplane Runway Game

Collect five toy airplanes (or make five airplanes as described in the activity on p.114). Write the numerals 1 to 5 on stickers and attach them to the airplanes. Tape a long piece of butcher paper to the floor. Use felt-tip markers to draw an airplane runway part way down the paper. Near the end of the runway, draw five rectangles for hangars. Number the hangars from 1 to 5 by drawing on corresponding sets of dots. Then let the children take turns landing the airplanes on the runway and parking them in the matching numbered hangars.

Hint: You may wish to make a rule that when playing with the airplanes, the children must either be seated or kneeling.

Airplane Dining

For each child place snacks such as crackers, vegetable sticks and dried fruits in a TV dinner tray. Line up chairs in rows to represent an airplane cabin. Then let the children sit in the chairs while "flight attendants" serve them their snacks. The children can hold the TV trays on their laps while they eat.

Orville and Wilbur Wright

Birthday: (Date unknown), 1787

Sacajawea

When the Lewis and Clark expedition set out to explore the West in the early 1800s, they were accompanied by a young Indian guide named Sacajawea, or "Bird Woman." The journey across the Rocky Mountains to the Pacific Ocean was filled with hardships, but Sacajawea was strong and brave. Carrying her baby on her back, she helped guide the men through the wilderness and make friends with the Indians they met along the way.

Leather Vests

Make a "leather" vest for each child by cutting a neck hole in the bottom of a large brown paper bag and two arm holes in the sides. Cut open the front of the bag from the bottom edge up to the neck hole. Hand out the vests and let the children use crayons or felt-tip makers to decorate them with Indian symbols or other designs. Then help the children use scissors to cut fringes along the bottom edges of their vests.

Indian Cradleboard

Make a cradleboard for "Sacajawea's baby" and let the children use it for dramatic play. Use felt-tip markers to draw a blanket-wrapped baby on a paper lunch bag. Stuff the bag lightly with crumpled newspaper and staple the bottom closed. Cut a rectangle (about 9 by 12 inches) out of corrugated cardboard. Bind the baby to the board by winding around a long piece of thick yarn in a crisscross fashion. Tie the ends of the yarn securely. Then attach loops of yarn to the yarn on the back of the board for shoulder straps.

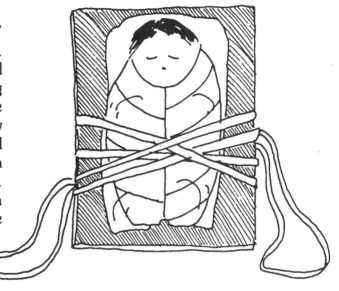

Fun With Names

Discuss Sacajawea's name with the children, explaining that it means "Bird Woman" in English. Encourage them to talk about the different movements that birds make. Then let the children pretend to be Sacajawea and do a "bird dance" around the room while you beat out rhythms on a drum.

Extension: Help each child choose an animal name of his or her own (Pony Boy, Bear Girl, etc.). After discussing the different names, beat out appropriate drum rhythms and let each child in turn lead the others in doing his or her own animal dance.

Guiding the Way

Set up a "wilderness" obstacle course in the room. For example, use cardboard cartons for boulders to walk around, a table draped with a blanket for a rock tunnel to crawl through, a two-by-four for a log to walk across and a long cardboard box for a canoe to sit in and paddle. For added fun, place teddy bears along the course to represent wild animals. Then let the children take turns being Sacajawea and guiding small groups through the wilderness.

Moccasin Game

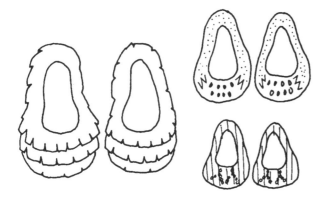

Cut pairs of moccasin shapes ranging from small to large out of brown paper. Use felt-tip markers to draw foot openings on the moccasins and to decorate each pair with different designs. Mix up the moccasins and place them in a pile. Then let the children take turns finding the matching pairs and lining them up from smallest to largest.

Nature Collections

Explain to the children that when explorers go to new places, part of their job is to collect new or unusual nature items. Then give each of the children a paper lunch bag and take them out on an exploration to find interesting nature items in your neighborhood. When you return, let the children work together to glue or tape their nature items to a large sheet of posterboard. Encourage them to group their items by categories such as leaves, feathers and seeds. While the children are working, talk with them about the different nature items that were found.

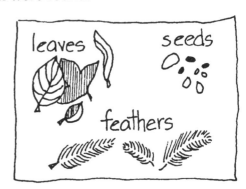

Sacajawea Song

Sung to: "Row, Row, Row Your Boat"

Paddle, paddle our canoe,
Let's paddle it this way.
Sacajawea will be our guide,
Let's follow her today.

Tramp, tramp through the woods,
Let's tramp our feet this way.
Sacajawea will be our guide,
Let's follow her today.

Climb, climb the mountain high,
Let's climb so high this way.
Sacajawea will be our guide,
Let's follow her today.

Now it's time to rest,
Let's rest our heads this way.
Sacajawea has been our guide,
We followed her today.

Let the children take turns being Sacajawea as
you sing the song.

Elizabeth McKinnon

Wilderness Snacks

At snacktime have the children make a pretend "campfire in the wilderness." Then let
them sit around their fire and enjoy eating
such foods as beef jerky, nuts and dried fruits.
If desired, follow up by singing favorite songs
or telling stories around the campfire.

Birthday: (Date unknown), 1864

George Washington Carver

George Washington Carver was a scientist who is remembered for helping to make peanuts both profitable and popular. When the boll weevil threatened to destroy the cotton crops in the South, Dr. Carver told farmers to plant peanuts instead. Then working in his laboratory, he made more than three hundred products from peanuts and peanut shells, including flour, cheese, instant coffee, dyes, wallboard and shoe polish.

Peanut Butter Playdough

Make playdough by mixing together equal amounts of peanut butter and dry nonfat milk. (Add more peanut butter or dry milk as needed.) Wash cookie cutters and any other playing utensils you wish to use and set them out on a clean tabletop. Then invite the children to touch, smell, taste and create with this different kind of playdough.

The Peanut Plant

Explain that although we think of peanuts as nuts, they really belong to the same family as peas and beans. Then use the following poem to help the children understand how peanuts grow:

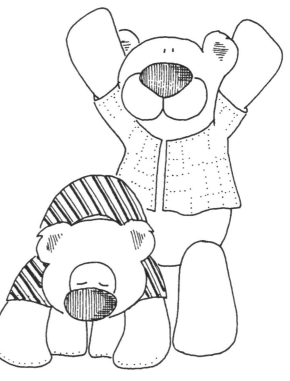

Up through the ground the peanut plant grows,
  (Crouch down near floor.)
Peeking out its little green nose.
  (Slowly start to rise.)
Reaching, reaching for the sky,
  (Raise arms above head.)
Growing, growing, growing high.
  (Stand on tiptoe.)
Then the flower starts to grow,
  (Make circle with arms.)
But it doesn't grow up! Not it! Oh, no!
  (Shake head.)
Down it goes, sending shoots underground,
  (Bend down and touch floor with fingers.)
And there grow the peanuts, plump and round!
  (Kneel and pretend to dig up peanuts.)

Author Unknown

Oil From Peanuts

Explain to the children that peanut oil, which we use for cooking, is one of the many products made from peanuts. To help them understand how the oil is extracted, crush a shelled peanut half on a piece of light colored construction paper with the back of a spoon. Have the children observe as the paper absorbs the oil. Then let them take turns trying the same experiment.

George Washington Carver

Peanut Games

Let the children enjoy the following peanut games:

- Use kitchen tongs to place designated numbers of peanuts in a bowl.

- Grab handfuls of peanuts and count together how many were taken.

- Sort peanuts that have been marked with different colored felt-tip markers into matching colored containers.

- Hunt for peanuts that have been hidden around the room.

- Have a peanut race, using noses to push peanuts across the floor.

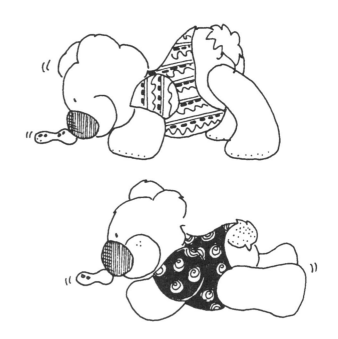

Peanut Display

Display peanuts and peanut products for the children to examine and compare. For example, you might include shelled and unshelled roasted peanuts, raw peanuts (available at health food stores), canned peanuts, dry roasted peanuts, peanut butter and peanut oil. If desired, let the children sample different kinds of peanuts. How are the tastes alike? How are they different?

Note: Eating peanuts is not recommended for children under age three.

George Washington Carver Song
Sung to: "My Bonnie Lies Over the Ocean"

George Washington Carver liked peanuts,
He thought they were really a treat.
He made many products from peanuts,
From peanuts that we love to eat.
Peanuts, peanuts,
From peanuts that we love to eat, to eat,
Peanuts, peanuts,
From peanuts that we love to eat.

Elizabeth McKinnon

Making Peanut Butter
Let the children help shell a package of un-salted roasted peanuts. Then have them chop the peanuts in a food chopper. Combine the chopped nuts with enough softened marga-rine to make a spreadable mixture and add a little salt. Serve on crackers, apple slices or celery sticks for tasting.

Variation: Make peanut butter in a blender, using 1 to 3 tablespoons vegetable oil for each cup peanuts.

Peanut Butter Ice Cream
For an unusual and delicious peanut treat, try making peanut butter ice cream. Mix together 2 cups vanilla ice milk, 6 tablespoons peanut butter and $\frac{1}{2}$ cup whipped topping. Spoon into small cups and freeze for at least 2 hours. Makes 6 small servings.

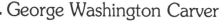

Activities, songs and new ideas to use right now are waiting for you in every issue of the

TOTLINE® NEWSLETTER.

Each issue puts the fun into teaching with 24 pages of challenging and creative activities for young children, including open-ended art activities, learning games, music language and science activities.

Sample Issue $1.00

You'll find the *Totline® Newsletter* an indispensable source of fresh new ideas. Page for page, there are more usable activities in this newsletter than in any other early childhood education newsletter.

"Out of all the materials on the market today, I find your resources are what I use."

"...The ideas are very refreshing."

"It's the finest magazine for the preschool teachers that I've found in my 12 years of teaching."

"For my money spent, I get more ideas from your newsletter than any other publication I receive."

"I love the Totline® Newsletter. I just keep finding new resources and ideas to keep me fresh."

Totline Books

Super Snacks - 120 seasonal sugarless snack recipes kids love.

Teaching Tips - 300 helpful hints for working with young children.

Teaching Toys - over 100 toy and game ideas for teaching learning concepts.

Piggyback Songs - 110 original songs, sung to the tunes of childhood favorites.

More Piggyback Songs - 195 more original songs.

Piggyback Songs for Infants and Toddlers - 160 original songs, for infants and toddlers.

Piggyback Songs in Praise of God - 185 original religious songs, sung to familiar tunes.

Piggyback Songs in Praise of Jesus - 240 more original religious songs.

Holiday Piggyback Songs - over 240 original holiday songs.

Animal Piggyback Songs - over 200 original songs about animals.

1·2·3 Art - over 200 open-ended art activities.

1·2·3 Games - 70 no-lose games to ages 2 to 8.

1·2·3 Colors - over 500 Color Day activities for young children.

1·2·3 Puppets - over 50 puppets to make for working with young children.

1·2·3 Murals - over 50 murals to make with children's open-ended art.

1·2·3 Books - over 20 beginning concept books to make for working with young children.

Teeny-Tiny Folktales - 15 folktales from around the world plus flannelboard patterns.

Short-Short Stories - 18 original stories plus seasonal activities.

Mini-Mini Musicals - 10 simple musicals, sung to familiar tunes.

Small World Celebrations - 16 holidays from around the world to celebrate with young children.

Special Day Celebrations - 55 mini celebrations for holidays and special events.

Yankee Doodle Birthday Celebrations - activity ideas for celebrating birthdays of 30 famous Americans.

"Cut & Tell" Scissor Stories for Fall - 8 original stories plus patterns.

"Cut & Tell" Scissor Stories for Winter - 8 original stories plus patterns.

"Cut & Tell" Scissor Stories for Spring - 8 original stories plus patterns.

Seasonal Fun - 50 two-sided reproducible parent flyers.

Theme-A-Saurus - the great big book of mini teaching themes.

Theme-A-Saurus II - the great big book of more mini teaching themes.

Alphabet and Number Rhymes - reproducible take-home books.

Color, Shape & Season Rhymes - reproducible take-home books.

Object Rhymes - reproducible take-home books about seasonal objects such as hearts, pumpkins and turkeys.

Animal Rhymes - reproducible pre-reading books using repetition and rhyme about animals.

Our World - more than 120 easy environmental activities.

"Mix & Match" Animal Patterns - multi-sized patterns for 58 different animals.

"Mix & Match" Everyday Patterns - multi-sized patterns for 58 different everyday objects.

"Mix & Match" Nature Patterns - multi-sized patterns for 58 different nature objects.

Available at school supply stores and parent/teacher stores or write for our *FREE* catalog.

Warren Publishing House, Inc. • P.O. Box 2250, Dept. B • Everett, WA 98203